GETTING STARTED WITH
EVALUATION

ALA Editions purchases fund advocacy, awareness, and accreditation programs for library professionals worldwide.

GETTING STARTED WITH
EVALUATION

PETER HERNON, ROBERT E. DUGAN, AND JOSEPH R. MATTHEWS

An imprint of the American Library Association
Chicago | 2014

Printed in the United States of America
18 17 16 15 14   5 4 3 2 1

Extensive effort has gone into ensuring the reliability of the information in this book; however, the publisher makes no warranty, express or implied, with respect to the material contained herein.

ISBNs: 978-0-8389-1195-2 (paper); 978-0-8389-9682-9 (PDF); 978-0-8389-9683-6 (ePub); 978-0-8389-9684-3 (Kindle). For more information on digital formats, visit the ALA Store at alastore.ala.org and select eEditions.

Library of Congress Cataloging-in-Publication Data
Hernon, Peter.
    Getting started with evaluation / Peter Hernon, Robert E. Dugan, and
  Joseph R. Matthews.
      pages   cm
    Includes bibliographical references and index.
    ISBN 978-0-8389-1195-2 (alk. paper)
    1. Libraries—Evaluation. 2. Public services (Libraries)—Evaluation.
  3. Library administration—Decision making. 4. Library statistics.
  5. Libraries—Evaluation—Problems, exercises, etc. I. Dugan, Robert E.,
  1952- II. Matthews, Joseph R. III. Title.
    Z678.85.H473 2014
    027.0029—dc23   2013017137

Cover design by Kimberly Thornton; image © Shutterstock, Inc.
Book composition by Dianne M. Rooney in the Charis SIL, Quicksand, and Gotham typefaces.

♾ This paper meets the requirements of ANSI/NISO Z39.48-1992 (Permanence of Paper).

CONTENTS

FIGURES, TABLES, AND TEXT BOXES

PREFACE

With all of the developments occurring today in evaluation and the link-
age of that topic with accountability, evidence-based decision making,
and strategic planning, the average library manager, especially if working in small organizations, may be overwhelmed and unsure where to
start and how to gather and use the resulting data. Further, most likely,
if that person graduated from an accredited master's program in library
and information science, he or she did not take a course, required or
elective, in research methods or evaluation research. Today, library
managers can hear and read about topics such as metrics, accountability, return on investment, and value, but without a background in evaluation research, they may feel overwhelmed and unsure how to proceed
and what the staff should be doing.

Getting Started with Evaluation guides library managers through
assorted topics: planning and decision making (chapters 2 and 4), types
of metrics relevant to the organization (chapters 3–5), customer expectations: satisfaction and service quality (chapters 6–7), return on investment and value (chapters 8–9), and using and communicating evidence
gathered (chapter 10). Chapter 1 introduces evaluation and chapter 11
provides a series of ten reminders for managers engaged in evaluation
and using the results. Each chapter includes directed exercises to help

readers apply the content, and the "Appendix" and "Selected Readings" sections at the end of the book offer answers relevant to the exercises and key readings, respectively.

For the evaluation topics covered in this book, we advise readers on relevant source material they can use, and we alert them about how to collect evidence. The goal is the presentation of strategies that do not require a sophisticated understanding and application of a complex research process. As librarians review what they want or need to know and sources of evidence, they should remember that they want to portray the library in the life of customers and communities, and not others in the life of the library. In other words, libraries need to view themselves from the perspectives of others.

Accountability focuses on planning, evidence-based decision making, and demonstrating to stakeholders the effective and efficient use of resources, financial and other, to meet the organizational mission and that of the parent institution or organization. Service or program improvement—better service to constituent groups—adds another dimension to evaluation as managers engage in benchmarking and apply best practices. Clearly, a focus on both accountability and service improvement is part of managing organizations in the twenty-first century. To do both effectively more academic and public libraries need to invest in management information systems that enable their managers to communicate with stakeholders important to the library.

In summary, *Getting Started with Evaluation* addresses two questions:

1. What might library managers do that they are not currently doing?
2. How do they do those things?

To help address both questions, this guide relies on the knowledge and experiences of three writers on the application of evaluation to the management of academic and public libraries. It is our expectation that our approach will make this book of value to library managers in academic and public libraries, be they directors, members of the senior management team, or at other levels of management, as well as members of governing boards and others wanting to adopt any of the concepts presented in a given library. We also think management and research courses in schools of library and information science will find the content useful.

EVALUATION

Librarians today are somewhat familiar with terms such as evidence-based decision making, accountability, change management, learning organizations, and strategic planning. Such terms assume added importance as library managers cope with decreased resources but elevated customer and community expectations, view technology as a change agent, and create sustainability, the capacity to endure and add value to the lives of customers, stakeholders, and communities served. Stakeholders demand evidence that the resources allocated to libraries and their parent institution or organization are managed in a cost-effective or cost-efficient way and that libraries contribute to vital outcomes set by the institution or broader organization such as those dealing with student success and faculty research productivity. Further, as many library directors and others realize, most libraries are undergoing a transition and, it is hoped, moving from "surviving to thriving."[1] As Barbara I. Dewey explains, "Transition affords a library organization time and space to prepare for strategic directions needed in our complex global world. In reality we are in permanent transition and, with the right approaches and tools, can grow and thrive in this dynamic environment."[2] Rush Miller adds,

> If our vision of the future is imperfect, it is better to be moving forward helping to define the future than to sit back, pat ourselves on the backs for how valuable we always were, and let that future move on without us. We cannot allow anything to deter us from creating the future for libraries that will maintain our relevance to the . . . mission of . . . [the parent institution or organization]. Even in a recession, we should seize the opportunities it affords us to question our traditions in light of the needs of our users in the digital age.[3]

Within this context, library managers need to monitor the organization's progress in making a transition to a vision of the future as laid out in planning documents while reviewing services and making adjustments as evidence dictates. They also need to go beyond anecdotes and assumptions while providing evidence of accountability, the obligation to be responsible for their actions and for the appropriate management of resources with which they have been entrusted. Accountability, therefore, should be a part of the organizational culture and the planning process: setting the direction ("what does the organization want to achieve?"), developing strategies to achieve that direction ("how will the organization achieve what it wants?"), monitoring performance ("how will the organization know how well it is doing?"), and, finally, repeating the cycle. Evaluation involves monitoring performance and using the evidence gathered to review and modify, as necessary, the direction set.

The Concept

Simply stated, evaluation is the process of identifying and collecting data about specific services or activities, establishing criteria by which their success can be measured, and determining the quality of the service or activity—the degree to which it accomplishes stated goals and objectives. As Peter H. Rossi, Mark W. Lipsey, and Howard E. Freeman explain, "The role of evaluation is to provide answers to questions about a program [or service] that will be useful and will actually be used. This point is fundamental to evaluation—its purpose is to inform action."[4] As such, evaluation is a decision-making tool that is intended to assist library staff in allocating necessary resources to those activities and services that best enable the organization to accomplish its mission, goals, and objectives.

Types of evaluation activities include the following:

- Program or service planning, which focuses on "What is the extent and distribution of the target population?"
  "Does the program or service conform with its intended goals?"
  "Are the chances of successful implementation maximized?"
- Program or service monitoring, which centers on:
  "Is the program or service reaching the persons, households, or other target units to which it is addressed?"
  "Is the program or service providing the resources and other benefits that were intended in the project design?"
- Impact assessment, which addresses:
  "Is the program or service effective in achieving its intended goals?"
  "Can the results of the program or service be explained by some alternative process that does not include the program?"
  "Does the program or service have unintended effects?"
- Economic efficiency, which covers:
  "What are the costs of delivering services and benefits to program participants?"
  "Does the program represent an efficient use of resources in comparison to alternative uses of the resources?"

Evidence gathered from evaluation is an essential aspect of organizational learning and is used for improving ongoing programs and services—continuous quality improvement (*formative evaluation*)—or reviewing completed programs and services (*summative evaluation*). That evidence can be used to distinguish between effective and ineffective aspects of the infrastructure (collections and services, staff, facilities, and use of technology) and to plan, design, and implement new efforts that are likely to have the desired impact on community members and their environments. The evidence might be quantitative or qualitative, and measurement, which refers to quantitative evidence, assumes the collection of objective data describing library performance on which evaluation judgments can be based. It is important to remember that "measurement results are not in themselves 'good' or 'bad'; they simply describe what is."[5]

Planning Context

A number of excellent works address the planning process for libraries, one of which is *Strategic Planning and Management for Library Managers*, which discusses the process and relates the components of a strategic plan.[6] The plan sets the core direction to achieve the institutional or broader organization's mission while factoring in the vision or the long-term areas of concentration. Box 1.1 identifies the core directions of a plan. For each direction, the library can identify activities that can be monitored on an ongoing basis.

Although infrequently used in libraries, a strategic compass summarizes the key components of the plan that will be of interest to library managers and stakeholders. The compass might be placed on the home page in a prominent location, and, if stakeholders clicked on any part, the key underlying metrics are identified and given. The purpose of the compass is to visualize key elements of a strategic plan, without having to read and recall a written document. The metrics linked to the compass should be accompanied by a brief discussion of their significance and how they enable the organization to move forward. Figure 1.1 represents a compass that could be easily tailored to apply to other organizations.

Box 1.1

Core Directions

Enhance the User Experience

Foster environments in which staff provide resources, services, and programs that support learning, teaching, and research.

Objective 1.0: Develop and manage relevant intellectual content, balanced across appropriate information formats, to support teaching, research, and service regardless of geographic location.

Objective 2.0: Provide assistance to users seeking information, and . . . using the library and its resources, services, and programs.

Objective 3.0: Coordinate a comprehensive information literacy program that provides opportunities to demonstrate student learning outcomes in support of academic achievement, career success, and lifelong learning.

Objective 4.0: Support access to resources and productivity by deploying and managing information technologies including workstations, the online integrated library system, and the libraries' website.

Objective 5.0: Create and manage a flexible, functional, and inviting physical environment that supports all forms of learning, discovery, exchange, and instruction.

Enhance Institutional Effectiveness

Objective 6.0: Provide administrative structure and support to manage and achieve the strategic objectives of UWF and the UWF Libraries.

Objective 7.0: Demonstrate the libraries' value to the institution and other stakeholders.

SOURCE: University of West Florida, Libraries, "Strategic, Core Directions, July 1, 2011–June 30, 2014" (2011), http://libguides.uwf.edu/content.php?pid=100407&sid=1590741.

Figure 1.1   Strategic Plan Compass

University of West Florida, Libraries, "Strategic Plan Compass" (2011), http://libguides .uwf.edu/content.php?pid = 188487&sid = 2380550. This compass is adapted by permission of *Harvard Business Review*. From "Collective Ambition Compass" by Douglas A. Ready and Emily Truelove, *Harvard Business Review* 89, no. 12 (December 2011): 94–102. Copyright © 2011 by Harvard Business School Publishing Corporation, all rights reserved.

Evaluation Questions

Peter Hernon and Ellen Altman view measurement in terms of eleven evaluation questions that cover a range of metrics.[7] Figure 1.2 lists these questions, which can be divided into three broad categories: those

1. under the control of the library;
2. jointly decided by the customer and the library; and
3. decided by the customer (see table 1.1).

The "how questions" under the control of the library include:

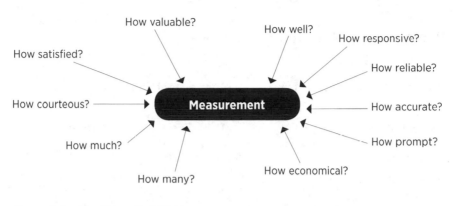

Figure 1.2 The "Hows" of Measurement

How much? The cost of providing a service should always be a concern for any library. All libraries (in fact, all organizations) are constrained by restrictions on resources. The resources budgeted for a particular service, be they personnel, space, collections, and so forth, determine in large part the quality of service that is planned to be delivered.

How many? Counts of various activities and processes help determine the "How many" questions. Daily, weekly, monthly counts of circulation, reference questions, people attending programs, number of items cataloged, and so forth, are examples of "how many." Such measures are often used to justify staffing levels by showing funding decision makers how busy staff members are. These counts are sometimes referred to as workload metrics.

A library can determine what percent of its community it reaches by comparing the number of registered cardholders against the total population of the community. Such a metric is often referred to as market penetration. Perhaps an even more helpful metric, sometimes called percent of active customers, compares the percent of registered library cardholders who have used the library in some way over the last month, quarter, or year to the total number of registered cardholders. In addition, use counts have been used historically as a surrogate measure for the value of the library.

Table 1.1

Components of the "How" Questions

LIBRARY CONTROL

How much?	How many?	How economical?	How prompt?
Magnitude	Magnitude	Resources used	Cycle times
Percent of change (compared to last year)	Change	Units processed	Turnaround time
			Anticipatory
Percent of overall change			
Costs			

LIBRARY AND CUSTOMERS DECIDE

How valuable?	How reliable?	How accurate?	How well?
Effort expended	Dependability	Completeness	Accuracy
Cost-benefit obtained	Access	Comprehensiveness	Performance meeting expectations
	Accuracy		
	Currency		Expertise

CUSTOMERS DECIDE

How courteous?	How responsive?	How satisfied?
Attentive	Anticipatory	Expectations met
Welcoming	Helpful	Materials obtained
	Empathetic	Personal interaction
		Ease of use
		Equipment used
		Environment (facilities)
		Comfort
		Willingness to return/use again

That is, the more the library is used, the more valuable the collections and its services are to the individuals in the community. It is not unusual for a library's annual report to include multiple use metrics touting the popularity of the library.

How economical? This type of metric, usually referred to as an efficiency metric, combines cost data with count or use data.

Efficiency metrics answer the question: Are we doing things right? The results identify the cost per use or transaction. Examples of such metrics include the cost to add an item to the collection, the cost to catalog an item (copy cataloging versus original cataloging), and the cost to lend an item. Efficiency metrics are often used to compare the operations of one library against the performance of a group of peer libraries in a process usually referred to as benchmarking. In this time of fiscal constraints, it is important for a library to demonstrate that it is operating efficiently.

How prompt? Time, the foundation for this type of metric, conveys the speed with which an activity or transaction is completed. Examples include the elapsed time to order and place an item on the shelf, the length of time to catalog an item, and the amount of time to fulfill an interlibrary loan request and to wait in a check out line. Time may be expressed in terms of minutes, hours, or days depending on what is being measured. Relevant data may be found in the automated library system in the form of a report or it may be necessary to gather time-related data using a sample of transactions.

There are several "how questions" that both the library and the customer decide. These include:

How valuable? The dominant approach to determining the value of the library is *value-in-use* as determined by the user of the service. The individuals using the service set the value of the service they receive. The benefits that arise from the use of the service occur first to the individual user. The possible benefits are categorized as being direct benefits (cost saving, time saved, new revenue generated, and gained information or knowledge), indirect benefits (e.g., leading to better grades in school, passing the GED, doing better on graduate aptitude tests, getting better jobs, graduating sooner, and generating new ideas), and nonuse benefits (someone can use the library at a later time or others in the community can use the library). The value of the library from a financial viewpoint is explored in greater detail in chapter 8, while chapter 9 discusses the value of the library from a nonfinancial perspective.

How reliable? There are several components of reliability, the most important of which is consistency. Customers develop a mental model of the quality of service they are likely to receive at the library. When their interaction with staff produces inconsistent results—some staff are helpful and some are not—the individual becomes frustrated. Another dimension of reliability is consistency of access: Do customers find the materials on the shelf that they are interested in, or can they locate an Internet computer that is not in use? And is the quality of information provided consistently accurate and of high quality?

How accurate? Accuracy is often presumed to be fairly high and thus most libraries do not actively investigate it. Yet, accuracy problems contribute to customer frustrations when they are using a library. Data about accuracy might be gathered about OPAC searches, shelving of returned items in the collection, responses to reference queries, quality of cataloging records, and so forth. Typically a sample is used to gather data to answer the question of how accurate.

How well? By seeing the library as contributing to the success and goodness[8] of the broader institution or organization, another how question addresses the impact of the program or service on its target audience: How great is the impact: the changes in the behavior, skills, knowledge, abilities, and attitudes of customers attending a program or using a service? This question more fully addresses outcomes. Impact evaluation provides feedback to help improve the design and content of programs and services. In addition to providing for improved accountability, impact evaluations are a tool for dynamic learning, allowing policymakers to allocate funds better across programs and services.

The "how well" question suggests how closely the library meets or exceeds its goals or objectives. Perceptions of how well a library is doing will likely vary (often considerably) depending on whether staff or the customer is asked. The most important consideration is the customer's viewpoint. Answering the "how well" question is, in almost all cases, a subjective answer, but, nevertheless, it is an important perspective.

Another important viewpoint for the "how well" question pertains to how customers benefit from using the library. For an academic library, the focus might be on identifying metrics related to student-learning outcomes. In a public library, outcomes might include the number of people attending instructional classes who pass the GED exam, the number of individuals attending a series of programs about entrepreneurship who actually start a local business in the 18–24 months following the last program, and so forth.

And the "how questions" that are in the sole domain of the customer are:

How courteous? Customers come to the library with a set of expectations, including those about staff courteousness. Customers compare their expectations with the quality of service they actually receive. If the actual service does not meet expectations then the customer is disappointed and perhaps frustrated. The customer might be pleasantly surprised when the quality of service exceeds their expectations. Over time, customers build a mental model of expectations, and library staff, with training, can become sensitive to meeting or exceeding customer expectations. Another aspect of courtesy is whether the customer is greeted when entering or leaving the library.

How responsive? Responsiveness can be considered from two perspectives: how well the library has thought ahead to provide solutions to potential problems before they arise, and how well the library responds to a problem after it has arisen. For example, assuming the library charges fines, can customers pay using cash as well as credit cards? Can they easily determine what copies are theirs if multiple customers are using a shared printer? Staff helpfulness in resolving problems or providing a service is one manifestation of responsiveness. Staff members who actively assist the customer in finding (or attempting to find) something in the collection are preferable to the staff member pointing in the direction where the resource is likely to be found (and leaving customers on their own).

How satisfied? The customer experience in using the physical or virtual library determines the level of satisfaction. Indicators of satisfaction include the use of a service in an ongoing manner (repeat business), the willingness to encourage others to use the library, as well as the inclination to be an advocate for the library. An important consideration for any library is whether to collect customer satisfaction data on a regular but periodic basis or on an ongoing, daily basis. Regardless of the decision, it is important that the library management team read each comment that survey respondents make. Many surveys will have 30 percent or more of the respondents providing comments in response to open-ended questions.

In conclusion, not all of the eleven hows are of equal importance. Those of greatest importance are perhaps:

- How well?
- How valuable?
- How economical?
- How satisfied?

Still, libraries have traditionally focused on "How much?" and "How many?" Subsequent chapters in this book predominately address these six questions, with an emphasis on the first four. Note that "How courteous?" and "How responsive?," to some extent, might be considered in the context of satisfaction.

Sources of Evidence

There are a number of ways for a library to gather the necessary data to answer one or more of the how questions. Some of the evidence gathered might result from the application of evaluation research and formal data collection. However, it is important to recognize that to identify the impact of the library in terms of outcome metrics, it may be necessary to identify the specific individual who has used a library service (e.g., borrowed materials, downloaded journal articles, and attended programs). The resulting data (with the unique identification number of the library customer) is maintained until such time as it can be combined with other data (e.g., student demographic and performance data) and the personal identification number can be stripped in order to protect customer confidentiality.[9]

Chapters 6 and 7 illustrate this type of evidence relevant to measuring customer expectations, including customer satisfaction and dissatisfaction. However, some sources of evidence for other chapters might not involve evaluation research and might rely, in part, on internal budgetary data (inputs showing the distribution of the budget to collections and services, staff, facilities, and technology; data that a group of libraries, perhaps ones perceived as peers, report; or usage data (outputs supplied by vendors, publishers, consortium, and individual libraries). If a library counts something, this activity may require evaluation research and a determination of the length of time for data collection, the accuracy of the data gathered, and the validity of the data collection process. It is possible to combine both budgetary and usage data and study economic efficiency such as by analyzing the return on investment. Further, customers or community members might be asked to participate in evaluation research to determine the value they assign to the use of the library.

In essence, the six how-questions can be addressed by using budgetary or usage data, or a combination of both. However, effectiveness and impact can be more complex and, when they address outcomes, the data may be qualitative and not so easily compared. Further, such data should not merely come from customer self-reports. In our view, librarians rely too much on self-reporting and far less on demonstrating what people actually do that they could not do before—the actual changes they have undergone (i.e., increased skills, changed attitudes or values, modified behavior, improved conditions, or altered status). Altered status might be gaining employment from attending library workshops about résumé preparation and employment opportunities.

Benchmarking and Best Practices

Benchmarking creates a point of reference against which something can be measured. Internally, benchmarking may be applied to evaluate services against performance standards, and it enables libraries to determine whether they are performing better than they did in the past. Expanding the focus of benchmarking, libraries might ask, "Are we performing better than our competitors?" Externally, with the collaboration of other libraries or organizations within local government, benchmarking addresses a new question: "Are we performing as well as, or better than, other units on campus or in local government?"

Benchmarking can be undertaken in almost any area of organizational activity. The basic requirements are that key performance variables be identified, measured, analyzed, and compared to provide a basis for planned performance improvement. Benchmarking can also be applied internally to reflect change over time and changes in processes in order to determine whether service to customers improves.[10]

Best practices, on the other hand, refers to best management practices, meaning the processes, practices, and systems identified in different organizations that performed exceptionally well and are widely recognized as improving their organization's performance and economic efficiency in specific areas. The goal is to reduce expenditures and improve operational effectiveness and efficiency.

Central to both benchmarking and best practices are change management, continuous improvement, and high-quality customer service. As leading organizations improve, they constantly look ahead and challenge themselves to perform better. In essence, they change and do not settle for the status quo. Benchmarking is not an end unto itself; rather, it should lead to the identification and enactment of best practices.

Concluding Thoughts

Planning is a critical activity for libraries as they embrace change and view the status quo as unacceptable. Anyone agreeing with Miller that the present, although full of challenges, represents an opportunity for change needs to create a vision of the future and work to achieve that possibility.[11] Planning for the future brings together those inside and outside the library; however, planning by itself is insufficient. Two questions arise: "How well is the library achieving that plan?" and "Does that plan require any adjustments?" Neither question can adequately be answered without someone carrying out evaluation activities and reviewing the evidence gathered to assess progress in achieving stated goals and objectives. Corrective action may be required. As a result, evaluation should become a daily activity, one focused on achieving the plan.

Exercises

Topic: Covering the reference desk is no longer an essential component of the work of a number of academic libraries as students use library services remotely or contact reference staff in ways other than approaching the reference desk with a question. Further, librarians are increasing their contact with students and faculty in course-related interactions such as through subject and course guides available on the library's website.

1. Given this situation what might be the focus of an evaluation study?

2. Is there a relevant literature on the topic?

3. If there is a decline in the number of reference questions asked, what types of questions do students and others ask?

4. Other than at the reference desk, how do students interact with reference staff? What is the number of these transactions?

5. Depending on the findings, are libraries pursuing other models of reference assistance, ones that provide service in a more timely fashion than the reference desk could ever provide and that focus on online contact with faculty and students?

6. The previous question links evaluation to planning. What are other models? Is one most appropriate to your library? If not, what do you do with the data gathered from questions 3 and 4?

7. Returning to the topic, which exercises are most relevant to a public library?

(Answers to these questions can be found in the "Appendix" at the back of the book. We encourage different members of a library staff to work on the exercises together and to discuss the results.)

NOTES

1. Brinley I. Franklin, "Surviving to Thriving: Advancing the Institutional Mission," *Journal of Library Administration* 52, no. 1 (2012): 94.

2. Barbara I. Dewy, "In Transition: The Special Nature of Leadership Change," *Journal of Library Administration* 52, no. 1 (2012): 144.

3. Rush Miller, "Damn the Recession, Full Speed Ahead," *Journal of Library Administration* 52, no. 1 (2012): 17.

4. Peter H. Rossi, Mark W. Lipsey, and Howard E. Freeman, *Evaluation: A Systematic Process* (Newbury Park, CA: Sage, 2004), 20.

5. Nancy A. Van House, Beth T. Weil, and Charles R. McClure, *Measuring Academic Library Performance: A Practical Approach* (Chicago: American Library Association, 1990), 4.

6. Joseph R. Matthews, *Strategic Planning and Management for Library Managers* (Westport, CT: Libraries Unlimited, 2005).

7. Peter Hernon and Ellen Altman, *Assessing Service Quality: Satisfying the Expectations of Library Customers*, 2nd ed. (Chicago: American Library Association, 2010), 37–46.

8. Michael K. Buckland, "Concepts of Library Goodness," http://people.ischool.berkeley.edu/~buckland/libgood.html.

9. Joseph Matthews, "Assessing Library Contributions to University Outcomes: The Need for Individual Student Level Data," *Library Management* 33, nos. 6/7 (2012): 389–402.

10. See Hernon and Altman, *Assessing Service Quality*, 47–50.

11. See Miller, "Damn the Recession, Full Speed Ahead." See also Peter Hernon and Joseph R. Matthews, *Reflecting on the Future of Academic and Public Libraries* (Chicago: American Library Association, 2013).

EVIDENCE-BASED PLANNING AND DECISION MAKING

ibrarians can no longer just tell stakeholders how important and critical libraries are to their constituencies; they must continually explain what they are doing and why, improve on the results that benefit their customers, and demonstrate how they successfully and effectively add value to peoples' lives. Libraries provide services via their infrastructure (collections and services, staff, technologies, and facilities). As a result, they need to provide evidence of customer satisfaction related to the components of the infrastructure as they meet the information-related needs of their customers. Because of their service focus, as operating budgets get tighter, and as new initiatives and continued funding are increasingly tied to accountability, librarians need to demonstrate the continual improvement of systems and routines undertaken daily.

Two principal processes involved in accountability are decision making and planning. Information informs decision making and the library's long-term strategic and short-term operations plan. Decision makers use information to ensure they are meeting customer needs and expectations, and they do so by identifying problems, considering alternative approaches, and deciding on adjustments to current implementation approaches or strategies in the ongoing effort to improve the effectiveness and efficiency of deployed processes. A planning cycle outlines a systematic procedure for indicating what the organization needs and wants to do, for the implementation of expressed plans, and for comparing actual performance to planned performance in order to determine success. Undertaking and sustaining planning processes help a library to introduce new services, improve collection development, and understand the information-seeking behavior and needs of customers in general and specific target groups.

The heightened importance attached to accountability requires credible and objective information. Evidence, oftentimes gathered from evaluation studies, is critical to informing both the planning and decision-making processes. Applying evidence-based information is intended to improve relevance and the efficiency and effectiveness of the planning and decision making processes.

Evidence-Based Library and Information Practice

Evidence-based practice (EBP), an interdisciplinary approach to clinical practice introduced in 1992, started as evidence-based medicine and spread, for instance, to nursing, psychology, and education. Evidence-based library and information practice (EBLIP) involves a continual cycle of improvement for how librarians work and make decisions, and applies the results to the planning process. Its basic principles are that all practical decisions should be based on research and that the research should be interpreted according to specific norms. Typically such norms disregard theoretical studies and qualitative studies and consider quantitative studies according to a set of criteria about what counts as evidence.[1] Evidence-based library and information practice, as considered in this book, applies Ellen Crumley and Denise Koufogiannakis's perspective: it "is a means to improve the profession of librarianship by asking questions as well as finding, critically appraising and incorporating research evidence from library [and information] science (and other disciplines) into daily practice. It also involves encouraging librarians to conduct high quality qualitative and quantitative research."[2]

EBLIP provides a structure for asking a well-constructed question that is important to the organization; gathering evidence; appraising the validity, reliability, and applicability of that evidence; applying the evidence to a decision; and evaluating the impact of the decision. Although the steps to undertake an evidence-based practice vary among EBLIP writers, this chapter offers six steps:

Step 1: Formulate a clearly defined, relevant, and answerable question which addresses a defined problem;

Step 2: Find the best evidence to answer the question;

Step 3: Critically appraise the validity, importance, and usefulness of the evidence;

Step 4: Combine the appraisal with professional knowledge and make a decision that applies the appraised evidence to the problem;

Step 5: Evaluate the effectiveness and efficiency of the results (the change) to ensure quality; and

Step 6: Disseminate the research.[3]

STEP 1

Questions drive the entire EBLIP process. For a question to be answerable, it must be precise or detailed enough to be conceivably answered by research. The wording and content of an answerable, focused, structured question will determine what kinds of research designs and data collection are needed to secure answers from practice. A model, referred to as SPICE, helps structure the question:

Setting the context: where?

Perspective: the stakeholder; for whom?

Intervention: the service being offered; what?

Comparison: the service to which it is being compared (note that there may be no comparison); compared with what?

Evaluation: the measure used to determine success; with what result?

An example of the components of a formulated question, using SPICE:

> In the Chemistry Department (*setting*), from the perspective of a university lecturer (*perspective*), provide links to electronic journals from a catalog (*intervention*), as compared to a web-based subject list (*comparison*). In doing so, a quicker route to identify relevant journals emerges (*evaluation*).[4]

It is a necessary and worthwhile endeavor to refine and reframe a question continually until it captures precisely the uncertainty the library wants to resolve.

STEP 2

The inquirer seeks existing evidence to answer the question. That evidence may be found in the published and unpublished research literature as well as from a variety of local sources of data. The early practitioners of the EBLIP process found that most of the questions librarians and information professionals ask in their daily practice can be grouped into six domains:

1. **Collections:** Building a high-quality collection of print and electronic materials that is useful, is cost-effective, and meets customer needs and expectations.
2. **Education:** Incorporating teaching methods and strategies to educate customers about library resources and how to improve research skills. A subset of this domain pertains to the professional education of librarians.
3. **Information Access and Retrieval:** Creating better systems and methods for information retrieval and access.
4. **Management:** Managing people and resources within an organization. This includes marketing and promotion as well as human resources.
5. **Professional Issues:** Exploring issues that affect librarianship as a profession.
6. **Reference/Inquiries:** Providing service and information access that meet customer needs and expectations.[5]

Matching the formulated question with one of these domains can help librarians decide where to search and the appropriate search terms they should use. This also allows them to focus on what they really want to know and to prevent the question from going in too many directions. Deciding on the domain in which the question belongs can point the inquirer to the type of research literature likely to contain the literature pertaining to the formulated question. Pertinent to the search might be library and information science (LIS) domain-relevant databases; subject-specific databases; journals, including scholarly journals in print and electronic forms; textbooks; monographs; web resources, including open access resources; and unpublished or informally published literature, including grey literature, documents found in institutional repositories, conference presentations, personal communications, and expert opinions.

The inquirer may encounter several challenges when searching LIS literature. The library may not have a subscription to the domain-relevant or subject-specific databases. Even if the library has access, there may be limited coverage of publication types, the inclusion of scholarly domain and subject journals may not be comprehensive, the indexing of the articles may be incomplete, the abstracts uninformative or absent, and the article may not be immediately available in full text. Additionally, the inquirer may encounter a confusing array of choices for how to go about answering the question.

The evidence published in the types of research literature found in step 2 may include:

Case studies, which describe a process, project, program, technology implementation, organization, library service, and so on.

Cohort studies, which track a defined population (the cohort) over time, perhaps in an effort to determine distinguishing subgroup characteristics. These groups may or may not be exposed to factors hypothesized to influence the probability of the occurrence of a particular outcome.

Comparative studies, which involve a systematic effort to find similarities and differences between two or more observed phenomena.

Data-mining/biblio-mining, which involves the discovery of meaningful patterns from data retrieved from automated methods. Bibliomining combines data-mining with bibliometrics, statistics, and reporting tools that look at patterns in library systems.

Descriptive surveys, which describe the perspectives or experiences of survey respondents on the questions that were asked in a predefined manner. Citation analysis is a variation of the descriptive survey method.

Focus group interviews, which generate information from a meeting of individuals. This method is sometimes used to complement the information gathered from other methods such as questionnaires.

Gap analysis, which involves surveys to identify discrepancies or gaps between individual expectations. Such an analysis is a central feature of satisfaction and service quality.

Narrative reviews (review articles), which is a review or overview of a subject resulting from an examination of the research literature. These reviews provide concise introductions to subjects.

Program evaluations, which assess the operation or outcomes of a program. Such analyses can be valuable in evaluating a program or policy at different levels in its development or implementation.

Randomized controlled trials, which applies control and treatment groups, with participants randomly assigned to groups. These trials can use individuals or groups. For example, a study could randomize different libraries to receive an intervention (e.g., access to certain resources).

Systematic reviews (meta-analysis), which identifies, selects, and critically appraises relevant research. The appraisal forms the study. Evaluators use systematic reviews to summarize existing data, refine hypotheses, and define future research agendas. A well-conducted systematic review helps practitioners avoid being overwhelmed by the volume of literature available on some topics. Without systematic reviews, evaluators may miss promising leads or embark on studies of questions that have been already answered. However, evaluators should consider study limitations and procedures (research design and methodologies) when they conduct such reviews.[6]

Evidence-based practice requires research to make good managerial decisions. However, other forms of evidence are also valid and worthy. Examples include local sources of data such as:

Customer feedback: Feedback alerts librarians to the fact that something may need to change or support what the library is already doing. Customer feedback usually comes in an informal way, via e-mail or face-to-face discussions in the library. Trends and needs may become obvious over time, and the evidence can be used to explore further what may need to change. Sources of local data may include complaint or comment forms, library customer-need assessment and satisfaction surveys, service quality surveys, external surveys which may have been administered by the institution, collected anecdotal examples of service impact such as letters and comments, and focus group interviews.

Librarian observation: Librarians observe things in their daily activities. This may be as simple as noting that all the computer terminals are busy and that there is a queue for most of the day, every day. Such observations tell librarians things about the environment and whether customers can effectively use the programs and spaces provided. Sources of local data may include consultations with staff.

Discussions/interactions with colleagues: Colleagues refers to those with whom librarians share and discuss experiences, as well as to brainstorm solutions and innovations. Colleagues observing or hearing similar types of things lends further credibility to what librarians may have seen or heard regarding a particular issue. Reports from colleagues may also contradict a librarian's perception and give pause before charging ahead with a decision.

Assessment and evaluation of programs: Assessment and evaluation are done on many different levels. Some institutions have librarians assigned to this role, and they may be responsible for data gathering on major initiatives happening within the library, as well as the reporting of library statistics. However, all librarians should evaluate the programs or services in which they are engaged in order to verify that desired outcomes materialize and program deliverables are successful. Sources of local data include evaluation forms for specific events, promotions, or instruction; collection analysis, such as a title-by-title evaluation of serial collections to make decisions during the annual renewal process; usability studies of the library's website; and instruction progress and student learning, including the frequency and types of information literacy instruction, and data on student proficiency using resources.

Usage data: Librarians already have much data at their disposal that can help with decision making. Usage data indicate the popularity of and need for certain databases, journals, and books. Data come from statistics provided by online vendors or publishers, in-house circulation numbers for print items, and other data collected such as the numbers of holds on items in the catalog, or numbers of requests for unowned items received either via interlibrary loan or patron requests. Librarians can also obtain usage data on particular in-house services provided or website traffic patterns. Sources of local data may include manually or electronically collected statistics and logs of reference transactions and federated searches, information desk services, and document delivery.

Organizational realities: Because each library's circumstances differ, local realities are a key element of evidence. Such evidence comes in the form of strategic plans, budgets, discussions with administrators, and keeping current with emerging issues within the institution. This is also an area where librarians may use previously collected data to make a case for resources and set their own priorities within a climate of fiscal restraint. Sources of local data may include internal workflow measures (e.g., time taken for document delivery and time to reshelf a book), cost-benefit and trend analysis, consultations with stakeholders, systematic performance measurement approaches such as the balance scorecard or a management information system, and benchmarking data such as student achievement (e.g., grade point averages, retention, and graduation rates).[7]

STEP 3

The next step is to analyze the quality of evidence found. The findings may yield an improved understanding of the question. The evaluator may not find an answer, but what is read enhances the comprehension of the issues and how to manage the situation better. Key to this step is critical appraisal, the process of assessing and interpreting evidence by considering systematically

- Its validity, reliability, and applicability for quantitative articles. Validity is the extent to which the results of the research are likely to be free from bias. Reliability is the likelihood that this study could be reproducible, rather than the results just being chance. Applicability is the extent to which the results are likely to impact on practice or be able to inform decision making effectively.
- Its credibility, transferability, dependability, and confirmability for qualitative research articles.

As everyone knows, not all research, even if it has been published, is good. Thus, how does the reviewer sort out the bad from the good? Although librarians may already have ideas on how to judge quality, several checklists have been developed to guide the reviewer through research articles in a systematic way [8]

STEP 4

Librarians need to integrate research-derived evidence with local evidence and professional knowledge, and use the evidence collected effectively as the basis for making meaningful decisions. They hold a great deal of evidence in their professional knowledge that is learned from formal education and training and progressively built from on-the-job experience over the course of a career. Types of professional knowledge include:

Formal and informal learning: Librarians who have a master's degree in LIS have a basic grounding in the theory of the profession. This education contributes to a common set of values, scope, and history of the profession, and provides a basis for future practice. Throughout a career, individuals actively engage in ongoing education, via such venues as conference participation, workshops, online seminars, reading of the literature, and conversing with other practitioners.

On-the-job training: Most librarians rely on the training and mentoring they receive from more experienced professionals. Mentors pass on their knowledge, experiences, and skills so that mentees can increase their professional capacity and skill in order to become better at their practice. Seasoned professionals also need to learn new skills to keep up with the latest processes being used, and thus meet the needs of users.

Tacit knowledge: Tacit knowledge is associated with those things that one knows but is not necessarily written down or that one may not be able to explain. Within librarianship, examples include knowing how to conduct an effective reference interview to help the person asking the question, or how to communicate effectively and build a rapport with faculty members. Librarians can explain to others some of the strategies used to do these things, but how to be successful in the overall process is more difficult to convey. These tacit skills are usually learned over time by doing and are the result of collected experiences.

Reflective knowledge: Reflecting on decisions contributes to professional knowledge and allows librarians to consider what went right or wrong, and what might be done differently next time. This process moves some of what is learned in a tacit manner into a more explicit, systematic approach, where learning, thinking, and making change are all contributing to professional knowledge.[9]

Factors that affect the applicability of the findings from step 3 to step 4 include:

The user group: How does the user group in the study compare to the local group of users? The practitioner will need to consider demographic factors, the type of organization in which the study took place (e.g., academic versus public library), size of the institution, age ranges of the participants, and so on.

Timeliness: Is this research current enough to fit with the present situation and the user needs of the local situation?

Cost: Is implementing an intervention feasible in the local work environment? Will there be sufficient financial support to carry through what is necessary to achieve a similar result?

Politics: Will the answer to the question be accepted and will it make an impact within the local environment? Or will it create adversity? One must definitely consider the perspectives of the major stakeholders under the category of politics.

Severity: How critical is implementation of the intervention? If the local library situation has a problem that requires immediate change, it may be more willing to attempt potential solutions even if the demonstrated benefits are only marginal.[10]

STEP 5

Evaluation often includes three elements: structure, process, and outcome. Structure relates to the physical assets that enable a service to be provided and configured (e.g., staff, facilities, and technologies). Process relates to how things are done within a service. Outcome, the most elusive of the three, is the effect that a service has on its users and the population from which they are drawn. Has a new service been introduced or an existing service modified as a result of undertaking the evidence-based process? In essence, has the process actually made the anticipated difference?

Plans for an evaluation should be stated at the beginning of the evidence-based project and address:

- What is being evaluated?
- How will it be measured (if the results will be quantitative)?
- How will the data be collected and analyzed?
- What indicates improvement or success?
- What are the goals of the assessment or evaluation?
- What is the time line for the evaluation?
- Who will be involved in the evaluation process?

There are numerous methodologies to gather evidence, but they can be conveniently characterized as ones in which respondents self-report and ones that reflect what people actually do.[11]

Step 5 is crucial in evidence-based decision making and planning. The findings from the evaluation, whether supportive or not, are used as inputs into the planning process. Did the action based upon the decision (step 4) produce the wanted or desired result? If so, now what? The successful outcome informs the planning process and may become an objective (an input) when updating the library's strategic plan. Library managers may decide to improve on the outcome (increase or decrease it) or to sustain it while incorporating it as an objective in the revised plan. Both a successful and an unsuccessful outcome have an important role in implementing the library's strategic plan. If the change intended failed, or if the success was less than expected, library administrators should still learn from the experience. The evaluation of the failed outcome informs the decision makers to exclude it from its planning efforts.

STEP 6

The evidence-based practice LIS literature points out that perhaps the largest obstacle in finding library research (step 2) is that librarians generally do not get the results published.[12] Librarians should make a professional effort to share their work with their colleagues. Inquirers will certainly seek to find citations to scholarly articles published in the LIS literature and indexed and abstracted in domain-relevant and subject-specific databases, and they often have immediate access to the full text. However, these traditional scholarly venues should not be viewed as the only outlets for evaluation projects. Librarians may make others aware of their work by:

- Publishing online in blogs, wikis, and personal or professional websites;
- Presenting a paper at a conference;
- Taking part in a poster session at a national, regional, or state conference;
- Conducting a workshop, session, or webinar;
- Participating in face-to-face or virtual discussion groups; and
- Using communications systems such as electronic discussion lists, e-mail, and social networking tools to increase awareness of the work undertaken.

A second important audience is the library's numerous stakeholders. Disseminate the findings using the language and communication channels in which the various stakeholders understand and participate. This will necessarily result in the findings being reported using a multiplicity of formats. For example, institutional stakeholders may want the findings reported succinctly in a paper format, while those who participated in the research may want to attend a face-to-face briefing held by the library. Others may want a more comprehensive report with details concerning the process and examples of data-gathering instruments in an electronic-formatted report e-mailed to them or available as a download from the library's website.

The point is that there are at least three audiences for an evaluation study: internal users, the multiplicity of stakeholders interested in the library and how it contributes to the lives of the library customer and noncustomer, and members of the library profession who may be considering the same question as developed in step 1.

Concluding Thoughts

Librarians make decisions every day, and short- and long-term planning are common managerial functions. In this accountability-focused environment, librarians need to become more data-informed in both planning and decision making processes. Evidence-based practice supports accountability by helping librarians explain to others what they are doing, why, and how successful or effective they are. In doing so, they demonstrate the library's contribution to value and impact. This evidence-based practice approach to data collection and analysis helps librarians to be more productive by improving their decision making and planning.

Obstacles concerning the profession's adoption of evidence-based practice include that it is too time-consuming when trying to manage a library in the new normal of decreased budgets, increased user needs, and the complexity of the six-step process. However, many librarians recognize the critical need to improve planning and decision making to ensure that all decisions are based on the best evidence available.

Library managers play a pivotal role in the success of the widespread adoption of evidence-based practice of planning and decision-making. The goal is to enable staff to apply evidence in decision making routinely. Creating an internal learning environment supportive of evidence-based practice includes formal training for library staff in research skills that builds on existing expertise, support and staff release time for research projects, and encouraging team mentoring.

The literature on evidence-based practice is both rich and growing.[13] As more organizations embrace evaluation and continuous improvement, they will find that data are important but that they are not a substitute for sound judgment. In other words, evaluation is more than merely gathering and applying evidence.

Exercises

1. Using SPICE as the structure, formulate a research question to learn about staffing the reference desk with paraprofessionals instead of professional librarians.

2. This research question relates to which of the six domains?

3. Where would you look for relevant literature (e.g., databases)?

4. What types of literature would you search?

5. What other evidence would you seek?

6. What criteria would you consider when appraising the quality of the literature found?

7. Based on the research question, what other factors may you consider when applying the evidence to your work situation?

8. Evaluation often includes three elements: structure, process, and outcome. Which element applies to this research question?

9. What would you consider to collect as data to help determine the success of the decision?

10. To whom would you consider reporting results from the evaluation?

(Answers to these questions can be found in the "Appendix" at the back of the book. We encourage different members of a library staff to work on the exercises together and to discuss the results.)

NOTES

1. Birger Hjørland, "Evidence Based Practice: An Analysis Based on the Philosophy of Science," *Journal of the American Society for Information Science and Technology* 62, no. 7 (July 2011): 1301.

2. Ellen Crumley and Denise Koufogiannakis, "Developing Evidence-Based Librarianship: Practical Steps for Implementation," *Health Information and Libraries Journal* 19, no. 2 (2002): 62.

3. Virginia Wilson and Stephanie Hall, "Evidence Based Toolkit for Public Libraries" (n.d.), http://ebltoolkit.pbworks.com/f/Handout.doc.

4. Anne Brice, Andrew Booth, and Nicola Bexon, "Evidence Based Librarianship: A Case Study in the Social Sciences," Conference Program from the World Library and Information Congress: 71st IFLA General Conference and Council (August 2005), 4–6, http://archive.ifla.org/IV/ifla71/papers/111e-Brice_Booth_Bexon.pdf.

5. Denise Koufogiannakis, Linda Slater, and Ellen Crumley, "A Content Analysis of Librarianship Research," *Journal of Information Science* 30, no. 3 (June 2004): 233.

6. Jessie McGowan, "Evidence-Based Librarianship" (n.d.), www.libqual .org/documents/admin/mcgowan.ppt; Andrew Booth and Anne Brice, "Appraising the Evidence," in *Evidence-Based Practice for Information Professionals: A Handbook*, edited by Andrew Booth and Anne Brice, 111–12 (London: Facet, 2004).

7. Denise Koufogiannakis, "Considering the Place of Practice-Based Evidence within Evidence Based Library and Information Practice (EBLIP)," *Library and Information Research* 35, no. 111 (2011): 44, 50–51; Marie J. Grant, "Evidence Based Library and Information Practice" (September 1, 2011), www.slideshare.net/MariaJGrant/evidence-based -library-and-information-practice.

8. See Virginia Wilson, "An Introduction to Critical Appraisal," *Evidence Based Library and Information Practice* 5, no. 1 (2010): 156. See also http://ebltoolkit.pbworks.com/f/EBLCriticalAppraisalChecklist.pdf; http://nettingtheevidence.pbwiki.com/f/use.doc (a checklist for appraising a user study); http://nettingtheevidence.pbwiki.com/f/needs .doc (a checklist for appraising information needs); and http://eprints .rclis.org/bitstream/10760/8082/1/RELIANT_final_.pdf (ReLIANT: Reader's Guide to the Literature on Interventions Addressing the Need for Education and Training).

9. Koufogiannakis, "Considering the Place of Practice-Based Evidence," 51–52.

10. Denise Koufogiannakis and Ellen Crumley, "Applying Evidence to Your Everyday Practice," in *Evidence-Based Practice for Information Professionals*, 120–22.

11. See Peter Hernon and Joseph R. Matthews, *Listening to the Customer* (Santa Barbara, CA: Libraries Unlimited, 2011); Peter Hernon, Robert E. Dugan, and Danuta A. Nitecki, *Engaging in Evaluation and Assessment Research* (Santa Barbara, CA: Libraries Unlimited, 2011).

12. Lisa Given, "Evidence-Based Practice and Qualitative Research: A Primer for Library and Information Professionals," *Evidence Based Library and Information Practice* 2, no. 1 (2007): 16–7.

13. See Sharon Markless and David Streatfield, *Evaluating the Impact of Your Library* (London: Facet, 2006). Additionally, all of the issues of the online open-source journal *Evidence Based Library and Information Practice*, published by the University of Alberta Learning Services, are available back to volume 1 issue 1 in 2006 at http://ejournals.library.ualberta .ca/index.php/EBLIP/issue/archive. This quarterly, double-blind peer -reviewed journal includes articles, valuable evidence summaries, and commentaries.

LIBRARY METRICS

For years libraries have collected and reported metrics about the allocation of the budget to support their mission and therefore the informational, social, and other needs of the community and to demonstrate the extent of community use, the types of resources community members use, and organizational efficiency. Such metrics as the amount of use of e-books and databases, the number of items borrowed and reference questions asked, and the number of items cataloged per week explain the library on its own terms (how it distributes the budget and the extent and types of community uses, both on-site and remotely). Stakeholders want data about such matters, but they expect additional metrics that explain the value of the library to the community served and how the library contributes to meeting the mission of the larger organization or institution. To do so, library managers have added metrics such as those about customer satisfaction and how the library contributes to the daily life of the parent organization or institution and to the life of the customer. This shift expands the number of metrics that libraries need to consider and report on an ongoing basis.[1] This chapter introduces the next three chapters on metrics by explaining them and illustrating different contexts: organizational, stakeholder, and institutional or broader organizational expectations.

Overview

Any use of metrics should be linked to a planning process such as that depicted in figure 1.1. The figure indicates priorities related to the mission and encourages the use of resources to accomplish specified goals and objectives. Richard Orr advanced the input-process–output-outcomes model so that organizations could organize a set of metrics that will meet their managerial needs.[2] Input metrics, which are usually counts of a numeric value, are the easiest to quantify and gather. They can be grouped into the following broad categories: budget and infrastructure (staff, collections and services, facilities, and technology). Data about library budgets and their allocation to the infrastructure serve as the basis for input metrics.

Process metrics, which are internally directed, focus on activities that transform resources into the services libraries offer. Because these metrics quantify the cost or time to perform a specific task or activity, they deal with efficiency and the question, "Are we doing things right?" Process metrics are generally either a cost-per-activity or a time-per-activity measure. A library usually compares its process metrics with those of a group of peer libraries in order to measure its efficiency.

Output metrics, which indicate the extent of library use, tend to comprise counts of the volume of its activities. Historically, these metrics have been regarded as indicators of goodness, meaning that, by being used, and, it is hoped, heavily, the library is effective and efficient. A multiplicity of metrics demonstrates different kinds of use—use of the collection (physical and electronic), use of facilities (gate count and program attendance), visits to the library's website, use of programs and workshops, and so forth.

Outcomes focus on customers and meeting the mission of the parent organization or institution; they deal with the extent to which use of the library changes customers—their knowledge, accomplishments, skills, and abilities. They allow a library to assess its effectiveness and to answer the questions, "Are we making a difference in the lives of our customers and the community?" For example, if the library offers workshops on résumé preparation and finding a job, for those in attendance did the résumé and other workshop content play a role in their getting an interview and obtaining a position? For further clarification, assuming a library has a goal of increasing literacy in the community, merely tallying the number of people borrowing books, the number of kids participating in reading programs, and the average reading level of the book borrowed does not indicate that participation in literacy programs actually raises reading levels. Such a metric should go beyond what participants self-report and show that their performance actually improved—increased by X grade levels.

SOURCES OF METRICS

Input metrics can be developed from the allocation of budget data to the infrastructure, while process metrics apply cost data to some measurable activity. Output metrics, for instance, might be compiled from aggregate data supplied by a vendor such as one providing databases. In other instances, library staff might compile data, and when they do, central issues are data accuracy and the time frame for data collection; the time frame shapes the extent to which the data are generalizable across a day, week, month, calendar year, and so forth. The time frame might be arbitrarily selected or based on some type of probability sample. Staff might also experience errors in data collection. Gathering data related to outcomes may require knowledge of experimental design and an ability to control variables and ascertain that any change is only due to the intervention applied. Outcomes, however, need not be quantifiable.

To determine the impact of the library on the institution or broader organization librarians cannot rely solely on an analysis of assorted input data. From that broader perspective, customer satisfaction (an output) and changes resulting from access to the library and its services (outcomes) may be important. This is especially true when managerial leaders focus on the library in the life of stakeholders and the institution or broader organization.

Library Perspective

In 1996 Peter Hernon and Ellen Altman suggested that academic libraries should publish a series of performance metrics that reflect the library's contribution to teaching and research.[3] Karen Bottrill and Victor Borden added complementary metrics.[4] Probably because academic libraries were not being asked to demonstrate their value at that time, few if any libraries took up the challenge and started to collect and report regularly such metrics. Hernon and Altman suggested metrics for academic libraries such as the following:

- percentage of courses with materials in the reserve reading room;
- percentage of students enrolled in these courses who actually checked out or downloaded reserve materials;
- number of library computer searches initiated by undergraduates; and
- number of references cited in faculty publications that may be found in the library's collections.

While most of these metrics are outputs, they do not deal with the impact of the library in the lives of students or faculty; they indicate the extent to which the library's collections and services reach different user segments on campus. As such they may suggest market penetration. Penetration is an important first step in determining the value of the academic library. It seems reasonable to assume that a library would want to know the proportion of students, faculty, and staff (or members of the general public in the case of a public library) who use the library, perhaps on an annual basis, as a starting point in determining the library's impact.

Academic libraries ought to collect and analyze the proportion of undergraduates, graduate students, faculty, and researchers who used the library during the previous year. They might want to know the percentage who

- borrowed materials;
- downloaded online materials; and
- used the physical and virtual collections.

With the exception of downloaded online materials, these metrics may also apply to public libraries, as do those that measure the types of services most frequently used. Still, a more expansive list of metrics, especially ones relevant to customers, appears in *Assessing Service Quality*.[5]

DATA SOURCES FOR BENCHMARKING

Libraries might engage in competitive benchmarking, a process by which a library compares its performance to that of its peers. That comparison might be of particular areas or across the spectrum of services. To make "best in class" comparisons, a library may draw comparisons to other service industries. To compare itself to other libraries, a library needs access to a data set against which it can draw comparisons. More academic and public libraries participate in nationwide statistics-collecting programs managed at the federal level which can be used for peer comparisons. The Institute of Education Sciences' National Center for Education Statistics (NCES), the principal statistical agency within the U.S. Department of Education, began a nationwide library statistics program in 1989 that includes the Academic Libraries Survey and the School Library Media Center Survey. NCES collects expenditures, services, and staffing data biennially from about 3,700 degree-granting postsecondary institutions in order to provide an overview of academic libraries nationwide and by state. Its "Compare Academic Libraries" tool allows users to compare one library (the library of interest) with similar libraries (the comparison group). For example, a user may wish to compare one library's total circulation with the total circulation of a group of libraries with similar total expenditures. Data can be loaded into Microsoft Excel tables for local review, analysis, charting, and graphing.

The Public Libraries Survey and the State Library Agencies Survey have been conducted by the U.S. Bureau of the Census for the Institute of Museum and Library Services (IMLS) since 2007. Data are available for individual public libraries and are also aggregated to state and national levels. Compare Public Libraries, a tool similar to that deployed by NCES for academic libraries, allows users to compare one library with similar public libraries.

The Association of College and Research Libraries (ACRL) and IMLS collect descriptive statistics through a voluntary census of academic and public libraries in the United States. ACRL collects academic library statistics through its annual Academic Library Trends and Statistics survey. It provides subscription-based online access to the resultant database through ACRLMetrics, administered through Counting Opinions (SQUIRE) Ltd. of Toronto, Canada. The online subscription provides access to ACRL and NCES academic library statistics (2000 to present) plus a select subset of IPEDS data specific to academic libraries.

NCES is also the primary collector and source for the Integrated Postsecondary Education Data System (IPEDS), a system of interrelated surveys conducted annually. IPEDS gathers information from every college, university, and technical and vocational institution that participates in the federal student financial aid programs. The Higher Education Act of 1965, as amended, requires that institutions that participate in federal student aid programs report data on enrollments, program completions, graduation rates, faculty and staff, finances, institutional prices, and student financial aid. These data are made available to students and parents through the College Navigator college search website and to researchers and others through the IPEDS Data Center.

Since the early 1900s, the Association of Research Libraries (ARL) has collected data on library expenditures, collections, staffing, and service activities.[6] ARL Statistics Interactive Analytics, a subscription service for non-ARL member libraries and others, enables interested libraries and researchers to expand the comparisons that can be made through application of ACRLMetrics.

Counting Opinions (SQUIRE) Ltd. enables subscribers to manage the above-mentioned data sets and to engage in internal and comparative benchmarking—noting trends over time—and to implement an evidence-based management system, thereby decreasing the need for academic and public libraries to develop and maintain a balanced scorecard, a strategic planning and management system that aligns business activities to the mission of the organization; improves internal and external communications; and monitors organization performance against strategic goals.[7] The metrics that libraries might produce include, for instance, "cost-per- . . . ," which is associated with economic efficiency. Other metrics might pertain to cost-per-database session, costs-per-content unit downloaded, percentage of population served with a library card (public library), workstation use rate, and attendance at workshops per number of staff members assigned to provide training. Customer satisfaction is an important output, regardless of the type of library.

PROJECTING LIBRARY METRICS TO THE INSTITUTION

Using ACRL and IPEDS data for college libraries, Elizabeth M. Mezick links student persistence to data on library expenditures and to the number of professional library staff. The strongest relationships, she finds, "were those between student retention and total library expenditures, total library materials costs, and serial costs."[8] Such an analysis applicable to academic libraries ignores output metrics that show the extent of use by students and the areas receiving the most use, and student and faculty satisfaction. Student persistence is definitively a more complex issue than merely the identification and analysis of some library input metrics.

Sharon Weiner, using the ARL Index, examines three indicators of library service (the outputs are the number of reference transactions, instructional presentations, and attendees at group presentations) and some institutional inputs (total professional/support staff, total library expenditures, total full-time graduate/professional student enrollment, total full-time faculty whose major regular assignment is instruction, and total full-time undergraduate/unclassified student enrollment). Her goal was to demonstrate institutional accountability through assorted input and output metrics, and specifically metrics not associated with satisfaction and organizational impact.[9] Once the issue of impact is raised, attention shifts to outcomes and how libraries truly make a difference in the lives of their customers and the institution. Although the literature on return on investment and value has progressed substantially since the first decade of this new century (see chapters 8 and 9), outcomes are absent from metric analyses. Still, this is not a reason to abandon such examinations; rather, this is a reminder of the limitations of such studies. As discussed in chapter 8, there exist some calculators to help libraries document their contribution to the institution, and they provide an alternative to extensive data collection;[10] however, they provide a partial or incomplete picture of the library's broader role.

One final study merits mention. John J. Regazzi uses data from the NCES survey to document shifts in spending, staffing, and use for a decade (1998–2008); however, data do not yet exist for subsequent years. Thus, the impact of the economic recession and the recovery is not documented, and would likely modify a number of his findings.

Nonetheless, others can replicate his study, in part, by comparing their library with a set of their peers. They can also document trends in economic efficiency such as by determining reductions in per-unit costs. The assumption, however, is that managers have access to post-2008 data.[11]

Institutional-Level and Stakeholder Perspectives

An important question that federal and state governments are asking is, "Why are higher education costs increasing so much?" As they address this question, they are increasingly focusing on affordability—the cost of obtaining a degree combined with the length of time-to-degree and the amount of student indebtedness to earn a degree. For example, the Center for Best Practices, National Governors Association, produced a report, *Complete to Compete*, which focuses on *completion metrics* as most important to measure; these include *outcome metrics* (the number of degrees and certificates awarded; graduation and transfer rates; and time and number of credits to degree) and *progress metrics* (enrollment in remedial education, success beyond remedial education, success in first-year college courses; credit accumulation, retention rates, and course completion).[12] When progress metrics refer to "success," the intent is to measure completion: the number who completes the requirement and advances to the next level.

Both completion and progress metrics, in fact, comprise campus-wide outputs, and they enable an institution to address questions such as:

- "What proportion of recent high school graduates enters postsecondary education and enrolls directly in a credit-bearing (e.g., non-remedial) course?
- Which college campuses are reducing historic and significant gaps among communities and between low-income and other students?
- What investments or policies are not yielding improvement in course and degree completion? Do they need to be discontinued so resources can be reallocated?"[13]

At the state level, there is a tendency to view quality in terms of the beginning salary of college graduates, graduation rate, length of time to graduate, retention rate, course completion rate, and separation of credit courses toward graduation from remedial education.

The type of metrics appearing in *Complete to Compete* do not focus on quality, when defined in terms of student and community learning. There is, however, a movement away from defining quality this way. Rather, quality is linked to student outcomes such as graduation rate and student completion rate (per course). This characterization is especially true of public education at the undergraduate level.[14]

COLLEGE NAVIGATOR

The Obama administration has developed the College Navigator, the purpose of which is to help parents and prospective students choose "the right school for the individual student while paying the lowest cost [to ensure] that the student graduates on time allowing . . . [him/her] to start . . . [a] career sooner and with less debt."[15] Incidentally, the Navigator mentions libraries, but only in the context of explaining what information the NCES collects on them.[16] Anyone using the College Navigator can develop a profile of prospective colleges and universities and then turn to the Department of Education's College Affordability and Transparency Center for "information about tuition and net prices at postsecondary institutions."[17]

Although the above outputs and efficiency metrics do not relate directly to the library, two central questions emerge: "Might (and how might) libraries contribute meaningfully to any of these metrics?" and "Do libraries have a role more with progress metrics than with completion rates? They might perhaps focus on retention rate, and how they contribute to it." Mark Emmons and Frances C. Wilkinson explore "the relationship between traditional library input and output measures of staff, collections, use, and services with fall-to-fall retention and six-year graduation rates at Association of Research Libraries member libraries."[18] They control for race/ethnicity and socioeconomic status, but do not rely on a wider range of outputs, metrics that view the library from the life of the student. They might have also examined the role of an information or learning commons on student persistence. Nonetheless, they provide a beginning to an important area of research and investigation.

Broader Organization Perspective

A public library might show its contribution to economic indicators, outcome metrics associated with employment and jobs (e.g., the number attending job-related workshops and finding employment as a result), and output metrics (e.g., the extent of customer satisfaction and market penetration (e.g., the number of community residents with a library card), as well as the number and types of recreational programs offered and data on attendance, the number of customers visiting and served, and use by types of resources. Additional metrics (inputs) relate to square footage of available building space, and the library might also report metrics on entrepreneurial activities such as those associated with having a bookstore or café or devoting space and generating some revenue from offering a passport service, a Dunkin Donuts, or a Starbucks.

ILLUSTRATION
A public library might set a goal of increasing the level of community engagement by 25 percent by June 2015. Objectives might set areas of community engagement that will be implemented over time, and the library can track the percentage of improvement and take corrective action as needed. Relevant metrics might relate to the number of rentals, visitors (new and return visitors), attendees at programs and workshops, and customer satisfaction.

Another example relates to donor relations and, for instance, setting a goal of raising $7 million by the end of next year. Objectives refer to the areas in which the library will actively engage in fund-raising and when the library will start each activity. Relevant metrics might be the number of donors, the average donation, and the number of large donations (defined perhaps as more than $500). The library might also track the percentage of donations over $50, the number of new donors, and the percentage of continued large donations.

Cautions

Metrics do not tell the whole story about a library, and they only comprise a part of evaluation. Evaluation may require the application of the research process to gather information useful for making service improvements and for demonstrating library accountability. Central to the research process for many libraries are quantitative data generated from surveys and qualitative insights resulting from focus group interviews. Unfortunately, both types of research depend on the memory of customers, which may not always be accurate; memory also fades over time. Instead, libraries might try to capture customer experiences and expectations almost immediately, before memory fades or becomes biased. To do so, they rely on online interactions such as those provided through the type of survey discussed in chapter 6. However, library managers must determine the percentage of online customer encounters, but not generalize the findings to all encounters, virtual or not.

More recently, academic librarians have started to study aspects of customer expectations, preferences, and use patterns through ethnographic research, which actively involves students in data collection. Most relevant for libraries is the concept of corporate ethnography, which is a branch of anthropology that involves trying to understand how people live their lives. Some of the methodologies focus on facilities use, and the results complement output metrics and document library use. One method involves a building sweep in which at predetermined times library staff observe users and document where they sit and what they are doing (e.g., positioned at a computer, working alone or interacting with others, studying while seated in comfortable chairs, or standing by the periodical collection).[19] Another study of facilities use might involve arranging an area and seeing how students reconfigure the space. Staff might take pictures of the reconstructed space and examine the photographs for patterns.

In planning new spaces or renovating already existing space, Jeanne Narum, director of Project Kaleidoscope, believes that too often planning "begins with the wrong questions," ones about what and how much will go in the space. Such questions tend to focus on things (e.g., computers or office space) and services (reference assistance and, in the case of information commons, the use of technology). Narum maintains that when such questions "shape the initial stages of planning, the process is skewed. You will not end up with the building that you need, that your students deserve." The initial questions should really focus on learning and what should happen in the space.[20] Clearly sweeps of the building or areas of the building provide insight necessary to restructure space to enhance learning.

Concluding Thoughts

As Christopher Stewart points out, ACRLMetrics provides a wealth of data that, among other things, characterize the distribution of the budget and reflect library efficiency. However, the examples he provides illustrate the library's contribution from its own perspective and do not reflect other perspectives.[21] Even comparing the graduation rate to total library expenditures per student does not address the ways in which the library actually contributes directly to retention and graduation rates, as well as to student learning. Further, do stakeholders see a correlation between library and institutional metrics?

The next two chapters go into greater depth on metrics. The first focuses on metrics useful for internal evaluation, making internal decisions, and engaging in internal evaluation. The second one, which examines external evaluation, expands on metrics useful for stakeholders (e.g., boards of trustees and accreditation organizations).

Exercises

1. Which metrics would your parent institution or organization find most useful?

2. Do those metrics characterize the library on its own terms or in the life of its customers or the parent institution or organization? In other words, how important are those metrics to customers and the larger body?

3. What story does the library want to tell? The answer to this question should reflect more than mere metrics. How might the metrics then be supplemented?

(Answers to these questions are found in the "Appendix" at the back of the book. We encourage different members of a library staff to work on the exercises together and to discuss the results.)

NOTES

1. For the most complete listing of metrics and the historical context of library metrics, see Robert E. Dugan, Peter Hernon, and Danuta A. Nitecki, *Viewing Library Metrics from Different Perspectives: Inputs, Outputs, and Outcomes* (Santa Barbara, CA: Libraries Unlimited, 2009).

2. Richard Orr, "Measuring the Goodness of Library Services," *Journal of Documentation* 29 (1973): 315–52.

3. Peter Hernon and Ellen Altman, *Service Quality in Academic Libraries* (Norwood, NJ: Ablex, 1996).

4. Karen Bottrill and Victor Borden, "Examples from the Literature," in *Using Performance Indicators to Guide Strategic Decision Making,* ed. Victor Borden and Trudy Banta, 107–19 (San Francisco: Jossey-Bass, 1994).

5. Peter Hernon and Ellen Altman, *Assessing Service Quality: Satisfying the Expectations of Library Customers* (Chicago: American Library Association, 1998, 2010).

6. Prior to 1961–62, James Gerould collected annual statistics for university libraries covering the years 1907–08 through 1961–62 (see note 1).

7. See Ian Reid, "The Public Library Data Service 2012 Statistical Report: Characteristics and Trends," *Public Libraries* 51, no. 6 (November/December 2012): 36–46.

8. Elizabeth M. Mezick, "Return on Investment: Libraries and Student Retention," *Journal of Academic Librarianship* 33, no. 5 (September 2007): 561. See also Lloyd A. Kramer and Martha B. Kramer, "The College Library and the Drop-out," *College & Research Libraries* 29, no. 4 (1968): 310–12; Darla Rushing and Deborah Poole, "The Role of the Library in Student Retention," in *Making the Grade: Academic Libraries and Student Success,* ed. Maurie Caitlin Kelly and Andrea Kross, 91–101 (Chicago: Association of College and Research Libraries, 2002); Stanley Wilder, "Library Jobs and Student Retention," *College & Research Libraries News* 51, no. 11 (1990): 1035–38.

9. Sharon A. Weiner, "Library Quality and Impact: Is There a Relationship between New Measures and Traditional Measures?" *Journal of Academic Librarianship* 31, no. 5 (September 2005): 432–37.

10. Cornell University produced one library value calculator for use by others; see http://research.library.cornell.edu/value.

11. John J. Regazzi, "Constrained? An Analysis of U.S. Academic Library Shifts in Spending, Staffing, and Utilization, 1998–2008," *College & Research Libraries* 73, no. 5 (September 2012): 449–68. This article also identifies the methodological weaknesses of using a data set such as the one containing NCES data.

12. National Governors Association, Center for Best Practices, *Complete to Compete: Common College Completion Metrics, 2010–2011* (Washington, DC: Center for Best Practices, 2010), 5, www.nga.org/files/live/sites/NGA/files/pdf/1007COMMONCOLLEGEMETRICS.PDF.

13. Ibid., 9.

14. See Peter Hernon, Robert E. Dugan, and Candy Schwartz, *Higher Education Outcomes Assessment for the Twenty-First Century* (Santa Barbara, CA: Libraries Unlimited, 2013).

15. *The College Navigator*, "Setting the Course," http://thecollegenavigator.com/.

16. "The average number of library staff per public school with a library was 1.7 in 2007–08, including 0.8 certified library/media specialists. On average, public school libraries had larger numbers of books on a per student basis in 2007–08 (2,015 per 100 students) than in 1999–2000 (1,803 per 100 students) and 2003–04 (1,891 per 100 students). In 2007–08, public elementary school libraries had larger holdings than public secondary school libraries on a per student basis (2,316 books per 100 students, compared to 1,432 books per 100 students).
    From 1991–92 to 1999–2000, the increase in college library operating expenditures was greater than the increase in enrollment; after adjustment for inflation, library operating expenditures per full-time-equivalent (FTE) student rose 6 percent during this period. From 1999–2000 to 2007–08, library operating expenditures per FTE student dropped 14 percent. Overall, there was a net decrease of 9 percent in library operating expenditures per FTE student between 1991–92 and 2007–08. In 2007–08, the average library operating expenditure per FTE student was $492.
    In 2008, there were 9,221 public libraries in the United States with a total of 816 million books and serial volumes. The annual number of visits per capita was 5.1, and the annual number of reference transactions per capita was 1.0." Source: U.S. Department of Education, National Center for Education Statistics (2011), *Digest of Education Statistics*, 2010 (NCES 2011–015), chapter 7: "College Navigator, "Fast Facts: Libraries," http://nces.ed.gov/fastfacts/display.asp?id=42.

17. Department of Education, College Affordability and Transparency Center, http://collegecost.ed.gov/.

18. Mark Emmons and Frances C. Wilkinson, "The Academic Library Impact on Student Persistence," *College & Research Libraries* 72, no. 2 (March 2011): 128.

19. See Nancy F. Foster and Susan Gibbons, *Studying Students: The Undergraduate Research Project at the University of Rochester* (Chicago: American Library Association, 2007); and Tracy Gabridge, Millicent Gaskell, and Amy Stout, "Information Seeking through Students' Eyes: The MIT Photo Diary Study," *College & Research Libraries* 69, no. 5 (November 2008):

510–23. See also Peter Hernon and Joseph R. Matthews, *Listening to the Customer* (Santa Barbara, CA: Libraries Unlimited, 2011).

20. Jeanne Narum, "Building Communities: Asking the Right Questions," Project Kaleidoscope (2008), www.pkal.org/documents/BuildingCom munitiesAskingTheRightQuestions.cfm; Scott Bennett, "The Information or the Learning Commons: Which Will We Have?," www.libraryspace planning.com/The-information-or-learning-commons.htm.

21. Christopher Stewart, "Overview of ACRLMetrics," *Journal of Academic Librarianship* 37, no. 1 (2011): 73–76; Christopher Stewart, "An Overview of ACRLMetrics, Part II: Using NCES and IPEDS Data," *Journal of Academic Librarianship* 38, no. 6 (2012): 342–45.

4

INTERNAL EVALUATION FOR PLANNING AND DECISION MAKING

Evaluation is an ongoing process that closes the continuous improvement loop: planning to implementation to the evaluation of what has occurred. With it the staff can plan and implement adjustments that will improve operations and services. Internal library evaluation is a systematic process of quality review undertaken within the organization for its own needs; the information compiled and analyzed from an evaluation informs decision making as well as planning and reporting.

Two important questions to ask when beginning an internal evaluation are, "What are the most important operations and services, and how are they to be measured to determine success?" Because no two libraries are identical, the answers to the questions depend on how the operations and services are directly aligned with the library's mission. An academic library's mission may be aligned with access to content in support of the faculty's teaching responsibilities and creating an environment of learning; a public library's mission may be as an adult and childrens' programming center as well as providing access to today's technologies that may be out of the reach of many of their service community members.

Another question asks if the resources targeted to support the library's activities are achieving their expected results. This question directly links the budget process to the library's objectives and activities as identified in an annual plan. In other words, are the inputs—the resources being applied—providing the outputs and outcomes wanted at the levels of use expected? For example, is the intended audience using the books acquired? This question addresses metrics covering funds to buy the books, staff to order and process them, the shelving space needed to house the books, and the equipment and staff to lend the book.

Internal evaluation helps library managers identify problems and strengthen accountability for results. For example, if the results achieved are not as expected, why? It may be that the service evaluated cannot be sustained with the resources applied. Or it may be that the resources applied are adequate, but the delivery of the service is not cost-effective; the costs far outweigh the benefits customers receive. With the quantitative and qualitative information collected from the evaluation about the cause of the deficit in achievement, and a thorough internal review and understanding of the reported information, the library employs an evaluative process to improve the effectiveness of its internal productivity and management and to improve service delivery to its customers.

Three Factors Supporting Internal Evaluation

Library managers are primarily undertaking an internal evaluation to learn about and understand the relationships within, and between, inputs, processes, and outputs. Inputs involve the infrastructure common to all types of libraries: collections, staff, technologies, and facilities. Inputs are often measured by attributes, such as their quantity; for example, the library has a collection of 100,000 monographs (input) and is budgeted $25,000 annually (input) to add or strengthen the monographs collection.

Processes, which convert the inputs into outputs, might be referred to as throughput. They are most often captured in terms of efficiencies, such as workload indicators. For example, it takes a staff person (input) thirty minutes to catalog a monograph (process), or books are reshelved within six hours (process) of their return.

Outputs are often measured in terms of cost, quality, timeliness, availability, and accessibility. They also include the amount of use and customer-expressed importance and satisfaction with the services provided by the library. The number of items circulated during a 12-month period is an output metric. Other examples include the costs to answer a reference question or to order and retrieve a returnable book via interlibrary loan for a user. As an example, it takes a staff person (input) thirty minutes (process) to catalog a monograph before it is available (output) to a customer.

The Internal Evaluation Process

Library director Sarah M. Pritchard has found that evaluation progresses through a series of steps:

- What is the purpose in establishing library services?
- How does one know whether and when the mission is being accomplished?
- How do library managers and staff make improvements that achieve quality and effectiveness?
- What is the ultimate evidence of success?[1]

These steps might be expanded. Robert C. Dickeson, a higher education consultant, recommends ten criteria to apply in a process when prioritizing academic programs; these criteria also relate to services.[2] Several of these criteria can be extrapolated by any type of library to create a useful road map when undertaking an internal evaluation (see box 4.1).

Quantitative mechanisms for internal evaluation include simple counting, transaction logs, budget and expenditure analysis, discovering direct and indirect costs (e.g., cost of mediated interlibrary loan/document delivery), and longitudinal trend analysis. Qualitative mechanisms include performance evaluation, interviews, surveys, the use of consultants or external review teams, unobtrusive studies, process

Box 4.1
Road Map for Internal Evaluation

History, Development, and Expectations of the Program

Consider:

- Why was the program established?
- How has the program evolved over the years?
- What are the institution's original expectations? How have these expectations changed over time?
- What is the degree to which the program has adapted to meet change?
- What is the degree to which the program has adapted the changing demographic characteristics of the institution's population (e.g., those living in the library's service area, college students, users of a special library's collection)?
- What has the program done to engage the population?
- What progress is it making?
- What is the visibility of the program?
- Has the context changed within which the program is expected to operate?
- Would this program meet the expectations for what the institution needs today?

Internal Demand for the Program

Consider:

- Is this program required internally, and why is it? An example could be the provision of reference services.
- What is the usage?
- What proportion of the population use the program?
- What would be the impact on other programs if this program was altered or discontinued?

Quality of Program Inputs and Processes

Consider the quality of the library's infrastructure:

- Staff, including their profiles (part-time and full-time) and numbers; degrees; years of experience; and recognitions and awards.

- Ratios of staff to customers; is there a viable balance?
- Is the program appropriate for the breadth, depth, and level of the identified need? How is the program subjected to meaningful analysis? Has it shifted its delivery to meet the changing needs of the users?
- To what degree has the program taken advantage of the advancements in technologies?
- How current is the equipment?
- How significant and current are the holdings in the collection?
- What is the degree of user access to electronic sources of information?
- To what extent are the facilities conducive to use?
- What resources will it take to bring this program up to a high level of quality?

Size, Scope, and Productivity of the Program

Consider:

- How many customers are being served?
- How many staff are assigned to specific services? What is the minimum number of staff required to provide the service?
- How many hours is the program available?
- How many services are provided (e.g., circulation, reference, interlibrary loan, equipment loans, and instruction sessions)?

Costs of the Program, and These Expenditures' Relation to Objectives

Consider:

- What demonstrable efficiencies in the way the program is operated are beneficial to the library?
- What investment in new resources will be required to bring the program up to a high level of quality?
- Can the library afford to be what it has become? In other words, is the program sustainable?

ADAPTED FROM: Robert C. Dickeson, *Prioritizing Academic Programs and Services: Reallocating Resources to Achieve Strategic Balance* (San Francisco: Jossey-Bass, 2010), 65–87.

analysis, job factor analysis, organizational structure analysis, and specific expenditure analysis (e.g., by discipline [genre] and format, and their relationship to an expressed need).

Data to Collect for Internal Evaluation

Evaluations depend on collecting and analyzing information. Libraries have been collecting data about internal operations and services for years. In its simplest form, a two-dimension model for internal evaluations focuses on the library's infrastructure and these three affective factors: inputs, processes, and outputs. The three factors, while often measured and evaluated separately, are interrelated.

INPUTS

Inputs are those tangible assets held, services provided, or operations/ productivity undertaken when each measuring period begins, usually the fiscal year. The infrastructure's assets included in box 4.2 are not exhaustive, but are representative of the common data that many libraries collect.

Box 4.2
Input Metrics Related to the Library's Infrastructure

Facilities

As an input, the facility describes the area(s) as available for use at the beginning of the measuring period:

- Number of facilities, such as the main or central library, and any branches including mobile facilities such as bookmobiles
- Number of staffed public service points in use; a facility may have a multiplicity of public service points which require staffing
    - The amount of physical square feet in each facility
        - gross square feet
        - square feet available for public use
        - square feet dedicated to staff operations

- a simple ratio is then available of public to staff space; for example, 80 percent of the facility is public use space
- Number of public use seating available
  - at equipment (e.g., computers, audiovisual viewing stations)
  - not at equipment
- Number of public seats associated with the type of furnishings
  - the number of "soft" (lounge) seats
  - the number of seats situated at tables
  - number of seats situated at individual carrels
- Number of public seats associated with the type of space
  - group study/use rooms
  - public use meeting rooms
  - program areas (e.g., children's story hours)
  - "quiet study" spaces
  - media listening/viewing areas
  - genealogy/archive/special collections areas
  - computer labs or learning commons
  - instruction areas
  - reading rooms
- Number of linear feet of shelving including
  - general collections
  - reserve shelving
  - reference collection
  - media collection
  - maps
  - government documents
  - new books area
  - genealogy/archive/special collections

Technologies

As an input, technologies describe the equipment available at the beginning of the measurement period:

- Number of computers available for use. This can be delineated into the various types of computers, such as fixed desktop workstations and mobile devices such as laptops and tablets. The devices can also be delineated into those that are available for use in the library and those that are loaned and counted as a circulation transaction (an output).
- Other devices available for public use. This may include fax machines, copiers, and equipment used for viewing content inside the library such

(Cont.)

Box 4.2 **Input Metrics Related to the Library's Infrastructure** (Cont.)

as audiovisual playback units, headphones, and scientific calculators. It may also include technologies available for loan and used outside the library such as video projection units, still and video cameras, and MP3 and portable DVD players.

Library Personnel

As an input, library staff are often considered the most important assets for undertaking library operations and providing user services. Staff are often expressed as FTEs (full-time equivalents) based upon the number of hours worked a week to be full-time as established by the library's parent institution (e.g., 40, 37.5, 35 hours a week).

- Number of total staff in FTE
- Number of librarians with master's degree from programs of library and information science accredited by the American Library Association
- Number of other professional staff whose duties require education or training in a related field, such as media or computing
- Number of all other paid staff who are not librarians, including technical and clerical staff
- Number of other personnel other than librarians and staff, such as student assistants
- Number of library volunteers who contribute to meeting the library's workload needs but are not paid by the library or the institution
- Number of years of staff experience in libraries

Collections

The collections available at the beginning of the measurement period are inputs. Collections are informational content (includes recreational and entertainment) in a variety of formats, the most common being print, electronic, audiovisual, microform, cartographic, and physical computer files. These include the number of:

- Monographs (titles and volumes) held by collection (e.g., general, reference)
- E-books (number of units)
- Current print serial subscription titles
- Current electronic serial subscription titles (including reference resources)
- Bound serial volumes

- Audio units, physical (e.g., compact discs)
- Audio files, electronic (number of files)
- Video units, physical (e.g., DVDs)
- Video files, electronic (number of files)
- Government documents, by format
- Maps
- Art objects (e.g., exhibited in the library, available for borrowing, in storage)
- Microforms (number of units)
- Licensed databases for which the library has temporary or permanent access rights
- Full-text journal titles available through these licensed databases
- Items in special collections or archives, measured in linear feet, cubic feet, or items
- Digital collections created or otherwise produced internally, and related file sizes

Other

This category includes:

- The recurring revenue received to operate the library. This is not the same as expenditures, which are outputs, because revenues allocated may be reduced during a fiscal year, often referred to as a rescission. Many libraries of all types have experienced rescissions since the beginning of the Great Recession in 2007 and at other times during the past.
- Number of public service hours planned or scheduled to be available when the measuring period begins. These hours may vary seasonally; for example, an academic library plans to provide more hours to be open during an academic session than when the institution is not in an academic session.
- Number of formal institutional and community partnerships and collaborations under way. Formal is defined as a partnership or collaboration that is mutually beneficial and may be based upon a memorandum of understanding.

A more comprehensive list is found in the appendixes of Robert E. Dugan, Peter Hernon, and Danuta A. Nitecki, *Viewing Library Metrics from Different Perspective: Inputs, Outputs and Outcomes* (Santa Barbara, CA: Libraries Unlimited, 2009).

PROCESSES

For internal evaluation, one looks more closely at how library person-nel use or convert the inputs rather than how the users use inputs; thus, processes are workload or productivity indicators (see box 4.3). Time and motion studies measure library staff workloads. Libraries learn about customer processes through self-reported use of the library, focus groups, usability studies, web surveys, and one-on-one consultations.

Box 4.3
Process Metrics Related to the Library's Infrastructure

Facilities

- Measures how the building and its spaces are being used, and when
- Library staff space being used and what work is being done
- User space, and what customers are doing

Technologies

- Counts how many public use computers are in use simultaneously
- Identifies peak times for computer use by measuring line queues for computer use
- Up time, usually stated as a percentage of time the integrated library system is available for use as opposed to time unavailable because of upgrades, maintenance, or repairs

Library Personnel

- Time to reshelve a returned book
- Time to catalog a newly acquired book
- Time to check out a book to a user in line (time in queue)
- Time it takes to have a book available for public use, measured from the time it is requested until the time it is available for borrowing or use
- Time to renew a book either in-person or over the telephone
- Time to repair a damaged print source
- Time to withdraw an item from the catalog once weeded
- Time it takes to answer a reference inquiry

Services

- Measure how people ask reference questions—face-to-face, virtually
- Learn what reference librarians use more often to answer questions—print or e-formats

- Determine preference or satisfaction with web-based training versus face-to-face instruction
- Interlibrary loan turnaround time
- Measure the length of time users are in the library

A more comprehensive list is found in the appendixes of Robert E. Dugan, Peter Hernon, and Danuta A. Nitecki, *Viewing Library Metrics from Different Perspective: Inputs, Outputs and Outcomes* (Santa Barbara, CA: Libraries Unlimited, 2009).

OUTPUTS

While emphasis in the past was placed on inputs, the examination, review, and evaluation of outputs have become more common since the mid-1970s. Although outputs can be evaluated at any time during the measuring year, they are usually compiled monthly and analyzed and evaluated at the end of the year (see box 4.4). Outputs can be generally grouped into usage, transactions, expenditures, and costs per unit.

Box 4.4
Output Metrics Related to the Library's Infrastructure

Facilities

- Physical space and room use
    - number of uses of group study rooms
    - number of uses of meeting rooms
    - use of specific spaces (e.g., number of people using study carrels, tables, group study rooms, soft furniture)

Technologies

- Number of uses (sessions) of public computers
- Pages printed on library printers
- Number of search engine transactions
- Number of accesses to the library's installed Wi-Fi system

Library Personnel

- Number of staff participating in development/training
- Number of staff development / training opportunities
- Staff turnover during the measuring year

(Cont.)

Box 4.4   **Output Metrics Related to the Library's Infrastructure** (Cont.)

Collections

- Number of volumes added, one-time and subscriptions, by format
- Number of titles added, one-time and subscriptions, by format
- Number of other materials added such as microforms, government documents, and audiovisual
- Electronic resources
  - number of log-ins to, or accesses (sessions) of, electronic databases
  - number of queries (searches) in electronic databases
  - number of full-text items requested in electronic databases
  - number of full-text items downloaded from electronic databases
  - number of e-books used (e.g., reviewed, checked out)
  - number of accesses of current electronic serial subscriptions
- Number of newly bound volumes
- Number of information items repaired or otherwise preserved
- Cost per item cataloged

Services

- Number of hours the library was actually open for use
  - number of days/weeks the library was actually open for use
- Gate count
  - number of persons who physically entered the library facilities in a typical week
  - number of persons who physically entered the library facilities by hour increments
- Circulation transactions
  - number of initial circulations
  - number of renewals
  - number of reserves
  - number of users who checked out library materials
  - number of circulation transactions by type of materials (e.g., children's materials, adult fiction, nonfiction)
  - percentage of total circulation transactions by type of materials (e.g., children's materials, adult fiction, nonfiction)
  - number of circulation transactions by format type (e.g., print, audio, visual, DVD, computer file, e-book)
  - percentage of total circulation transactions by format type (e.g., print, audio, visual, DVD, computer file, e-book)
  - number of circulation transactions by physical location
  - cost per circulation transaction
- Reference transactions
  - number answered, and by delivery methodology (e.g., electronic, face-to-face, telephone). An interesting measure

is the percentage of electronic reference transactions of total reference activity
- number of consultations by time expended to answer (e.g., less than 20 minutes, greater than 20 minutes)
- number of reference queries, by location
- cost per reference question answered
- Interlibrary loan transactions
  - number of items borrowed from other libraries
  - number of items loaned to other libraries
  - interlibrary loan fill rate
  - documents delivered to library or user via commercial services
  - cost per loaned resource via interlibrary loan
  - cost per borrowed resource via interlibrary loan
- Presentation transactions
  - number of presentations given by a library staff person, in or out of library
  - number of library orientations conducted
  - number of persons attending presentations and orientations
- Program transactions
  - number of library programs
  - attendance at programs by type of program, such as summer reading
  - attendance at programs by type of user, such as children, students, adults
- Instruction transactions
  - number of librarian-led instructions conducted, and by location
  - number of persons attending librarian-led instructions, and by location
  - number of uses of library help guides
  - number of uses of online tutorials
- Borrowers
  - number of registered borrowers
  - percentage of registered borrowers to service population
- Percentage of uptime availability of integrated library system
- Virtual visits
  - number of virtual visits to library's website
  - number of virtual visits to library's catalog
  - number of virtual visits to collections created by the library's digitization activities
  - the month, week, day, and time of the virtual visits
- Support provided to users
  - number of user contacts in person

(Cont.)

Box 4.4 **Output Metrics Related to the Library's Infrastructure** (Cont.)

- number of user contacts via online services
- number of interactions to support faculty teaching
- number of interactions to support faculty research
- number of interactions to support faculty scholarship
- number of interactions to support students taking formal courses through distance education
- Number of formal partnerships and collaborations within the institutional structure for which activity occurred
- Number of formal partnerships and collaborations within the external community for which activity occurred

Expenditures

- Total of library expenditures
- Library personnel
  - salaries and wages of professional staff
  - salaries and wages of support staff
  - salaries and wages of student assistants
  - employee benefits
- Collections
  - print materials, one time
  - electronic materials, one time (e-books)
  - other materials such as microforms, government documents, and audiovisual, one time
  - print materials, current serial subscriptions
  - electronic materials, current serial subscriptions
- Access fees
  - electronic reference sources and aggregation services
  - average cost per resource added, by format
- Other direct expenditures
  - other operating expenditures, such as supplies, equipment, repairs, maintenance of the facility, memberships
  - document delivery/interlibrary loan such as fees for photocopying, royalties, access fees
  - preservation, including binding and rebinding, materials conservation, deacidification, and so on.
  - computer hardware and software
  - bibliographic utilities, networks, and consortia
- Capital expenditures, the level of which is usually defined at the institutional level

A more comprehensive list is found in the appendixes of Robert E. Dugan, Peter Hernon, and Danuta A. Nitecki, *Viewing Library Metrics from Different Perspective: Inputs, Outputs and Outcomes* (Santa Barbara, CA: Libraries Unlimited, 2009).

Satisfaction, an important area to collect data because stakeholders as well as library managers want to know about it, might be measured by means of surveys, e-mail messages, suggestion boxes, or face-to-face. Chapters 6 amplifies on satisfaction, but, suffice to say, libraries might examine it internally (the satisfaction of library employees) or externally (library customers). It is important to conduct both types of satisfaction studies because staff cannot generate external satisfaction unless they express satisfaction or contentment as well. Further, an analysis of satisfaction should not exclude complaints (number and patterns) and speedy resolution of those complaints. After all, complaints are an opportunity to improve customer service.[3]

What to Evaluate Internally

An internal evaluation is primarily used to inform library managers about resources, services, programs, and operations within the organization. Data compiled as an input, process, or output yield descriptive quantitative information such as how many people attended programs during a fiscal or calendar year. This information becomes more useful when data that have been consistently counted and compiled over years are available, and reviewed longitudinally.

Library managers may also use internal evaluations to review and link inputs, processes, or outputs, using qualitative data to inform decisions concerning operations, services, and staff productivity. For example, an internal evaluation might align decreasing gate counts (output) with the decrease in the number of scheduled library hours open (input). Aware of this information, library managers may decide to rationalize the decreasing gate counts and library hours open as the reality of the current budget situation and then lower stakeholder expectations concerning the need to increase gate counts annually, or they may try to increase gate counts by increasing or otherwise altering scheduled hours open.

Box 4.5 offers examples of metrics that are useful when undertaking internal evaluations. Most combine two or more input and/or output metrics, such as *gate counts* and the number of hours the library was actually opened during the year, to create the *gate count per hours open* (calculated by dividing the annual gate count by the number of hours actually open during the year; this metric may also be calculated by the day, week, or month as well as the entire year). Additionally, many of the metrics used for internal evaluations lend themselves to longitudinal review. Creating a line chart of the *annual gate count per hours open* over time, such as five to ten years, will illustrate a trend.

Box 4.5
Metrics for Internal Evaluation

Physical and Virtual Visits

- Physical visits to the library per capita (e.g., geopolitical resident, direct service users, students, faculty) are a very useful measure, especially longitudinal, and when evaluated along with other quantitative measures such as the number of hours open during the week and the number of days and weeks open during the measuring year.
- Gate count
    - per hour open
    - hours open/service population (e.g., geopolitical resident, library users, students) scaled to 1,000 capita
    - per FTE library staff
- Percentage of virtual visits of all library visits. This measure helps the library manager to understand the virtual use of the library versus the physical use of the library. Tracked over years, the library may discover important changes in how users come to the library, and when. It may be that a significant portion of users virtually visit the library when the physical library is closed. A conclusion could be drawn, then, that the accessibility of the library and use of its resources has increased even when the library is physically closed.

Facilities

- Gross square feet of public space available per capita (the service population, e.g., geopolitical resident, direct service users, students, faculty)
- Gross square feet of staff space available per FTE staff
- Number of public seats available per capita (the service population) total
    - number of public seats available per capita at equipment
    - number of public seats available per capita not at equipment
- Ratio of linear feet of shelving by material types shelved

- Ratio of linear feet of shelving in use to empty shelving; provides a growth-to-capacity measure
- Percentage of use versus nonuse of:
    - tables
    - individual carrels
    - group study/use rooms
    - meeting rooms
    - program areas (e.g., children's story hours)
    - "quiet study" spaces
    - media listening/viewing areas,
    - genealogy/archive/special collections areas
    - computer labs or learning commons
    - instruction areas
    - reading rooms
- Customer demographics and use
- Proportion of the service population (e.g., geopolitical resident, direct service users, student, faculty) who:
    - used the library
    - borrowed materials
    - downloaded online materials
    - used the physical and virtual collections
- Number of public service staff per capita (service population)

Circulation

- Circulation transactions per capita (service population) are a very useful measure, especially longitudinal over five to ten years.
- Circulation transactions per hour open
- Initial circulation transactions related to time inform the library manager as to staffing needs
    - the busiest day of the week
    - the busiest hour of the day
    - the busiest month of the year
- Circulation transactions
    - per 1,000 capita (service population)
    - per FTE library staff
- Demographics of the user checking out materials; knowing who is checking out materials—students, children, adults, senior citizens—provides rich information. A library may revise the items it acquires or otherwise makes available based upon changing user demographics.

(Cont.)

Box 4.5 **Metrics for Internal Evaluation** (Cont.)

Collections

- Percentage of collection by formats (e.g., print monographs; e-journal titles)
- Percentage of electronic books to all monographs. Has the ratio of e-books to print monographs changed over the past five years?
- Percentage of electronic journals titles to print serial subscription titles. Has the ratio of e-journals to print journal titles changed over the past five years?
- E-journal use and use of interlibrary loan. Have the introduction and increasing use of e-journals decreased interlibrary loan requests for articles?
- Use and cost of aggregated electronic databases. What is the cost per use (based upon access fees and/or licenses) for each aggregated database?
- Use and cost of electronic full-text journals by title. What is the cost per use by journal title?
- Use and cost per access (based upon access fees and/or licenses) of current electronic serial subscriptions
- Print and electronic serials use statistics. These statistics may facilitate print collection decisions. Does the library need to purchase journal titles in both print and electronic formats; for example, is the print journal's use high enough to justify its continuing costs? This is also related to the "big deals versus a la carte." Are the uses of the journals included in electronic collections of titles from publishers worth the cost of the aggregation, or should the library purchase access to just those discrete electronic titles that have proven use?
- Age of the collection (copyright date) by call number ranges
- Collection use by call number ranges

Expenditures

- The percentage expended for collections, library personnel, and other expenses as a ratio of all expenditures (e.g., 20 percent was expended for collections, 70 percent on personnel, and 10 percent on other expenditures). Knowing these ratios is quite useful when aligned with the library's strategic plan. For example, library managers may conclude that the ratio of expenditures for collections is too low. This particular ratio can then be affected by increasing the expenditures on collections or, conversely, decreasing the expenditures for library personnel.
- Expenditures for collections by format as a ratio, and how the ratio has changed over the past years (e.g., ten years ago 25 percent of the library's collection expenditures was on print monographs; today print monographs are 10 percent of the library's collection expenditures).
  - percentage of expenditures for print resources versus electronic resources

- percentage of expenditures for serial formats to monographs and other one-time expenditures
- Percentage expended on content purchased and owned versus content annually licensed and would be lost if the lease is not renewed
- Economies of scale as measured by the percentage of resources expended for materials via consortia. This is an affordability measure; library managers can learn how much the library is taking advantage of consortia pricing. If the library is not realizing good economies of scale, library managers may decide to pursue memberships in other consortia.
- Percentage of expenditures on cloud computing; this cost is likely to increase in the future as libraries access an increasing amount of information content "in the cloud"
- Cost of the library's digital collection construction and management
- Library expenditures as a percentage of the institution's expenditures

Technologies

- Ratio of public computer workstation to service population (e.g., geopolitical resident, direct service users, students, and faculty)
- Public Internet computer use per capita (service population)
- Number of service population (e.g., geopolitical resident, direct service users, students, faculty) per public workstation
- The frequency that all computers are in use and a queue forms. The library manager may use this evaluative information to rationalize a request for additional workstations or to place a use time limit on the machines at certain times of the day or at all times the computers are available for use.

Other (Examples)

- Program attendance per capita (service population). This measure is useful if the library has focused on increasing programs and wants to learn if the effort meets the success measures identified in the strategic plan.
- Partnerships and collaborations within the institutional structure or in the external community. Measures involved would identify the partnerships, what is being accomplished, and whether or not the partnership and the effort are mutually beneficial and sustainable.
- Information about borrowing via interlibrary loan is reviewed and the information is used to inform decisions concerning collection development in selective areas of borrowing.

A more comprehensive list is found in the appendixes of Robert E. Dugan, Peter Hernon, and Danuta A. Nitecki, *Viewing Library Metrics from Different Perspective: Inputs, Outputs and Outcomes* (Santa Barbara, CA: Libraries Unlimited, 2009).

Internal Evaluation and External Comparisons

The metrics discussed in this chapter relate to evaluations using data collected and analyzed internally to learn about the current status of services, programs, and operations; to identify trends when the measures are viewed longitudinally; and to inform decision making. Additionally, several of the data elements identified and compiled may also be used for external peer and aspirant comparisons: "How does my library match up with other libraries concerning this metric?" Such comparisons, also occasionally referred to as benchmarks or best practices, do not measure quality but certainly help managers to understand the library's relative position in comparison to the average for groups of libraries.

When making comparisons between or among libraries it is *most important* to ensure that the data or metrics used from the peer or aspirant libraries are reliable; for example, the metrics being compared adhere to the same definitions. If not, the data are more likely to be as different as "apples and oranges," and the comparisons are flawed. The previous chapter discusses reliable sources of academic library data, including the ACRLMetrics program at the Association of College and Research Libraries. Because not all libraries participate in national-level data collection programs, managers should be cautious when comparing and evaluating data from peer and aspirant libraries not participating in a recognized national level program.

Basic benchmarks used by the *LJ* Index of Public Library Service to measure the levels of public library service delivery (service outputs and expenditures) relative to peer libraries nationally include circulation per capita, visits per capita, program attendance per capita, and public Internet computer use per capita.[4] Many of the benchmark comparisons for peer and aspirant academic libraries depicted in box 4.6 may be extrapolated to the environment of public libraries and used as feasible (e.g., substitute "student FTE" with the service population or a demographic of the service population such as a young adult).

Box 4.6
Benchmarking Metrics

Services

- Total circulation per 1,000 enrolled student FTE
- Number of reference transactions per enrolled student FTE
- Number of interlibrary loans loaned per enrolled student FTE
- Number of interlibrary loans borrowed per enrolled student FTE
- Ratio of items loaned to items borrowed (determines if the library is a net lender or net borrower)
- Librarian-led instructional sessions per enrolled student FTE

Collections

- Number of volumes held per enrolled student FTE, by format
- Number of titles held per enrolled student FTE, by format
- Number of serial subscriptions per enrolled student FTE
- Number of e-journal subscriptions per enrolled student FTE
- Holdings per circulation
- Circulation per holdings

Expenditures per Enrolled Student FTE

- Total operating expenditures per enrolled student FTE
- Total library resources (collections) expenditures per student FTE
- Monograph expenditures per enrolled student FTE
- Serials expenditures per enrolled student FTE
- Total electronic materials expenditures per enrolled student FTE
- Other library materials expenditures per enrolled student FTE
- Total staff expenditures per enrolled student FTE
- Salaries and wages
    - professional staff per enrolled student FTE
    - support staff per enrolled student FTE
    - student assistants per enrolled student FTE
- Other library direct expenditures per enrolled student FTE

Expenditure Percentages

- Percentage of operating expenditures on
    - collection materials
    - staff expenditures
    - other operating expenditures

(Cont.)

Box 4.6 **Benchmarking Metrics** (Cont.)

Library Personnel Staffing

- Number of total staff in FTE
- Number of professional staff in FTE
- Number of support staff in FTE
- Number of student assistants in FTE
- Percentage of professional staff to total staff
- Percentage of support staff to total staff
- Percentage of student assistants to total staff
- Number of enrolled students per FTE staff (full-time and part-time undergraduate and graduate)
- Number of library staff per 1,000 students in both FTE and head count
- Ratio of FTE library staff to combined faculty and student FTE

To the list of metrics covered in the table, an additional one might relate to processes and include cost per hours open (total expenditures divided by total hours open). This metric might also be calculated with only library personnel costs or may include other operating costs as well.

Concluding Thoughts

The evaluation of internal library operations and services is an essential part of the management process and critical for library managers to do. There is no shortage of data that might be collected and compiled for evaluative analysis. Internal evaluations conducted by library managers use a systematic process to learn about the status of the library's infrastructure as related to its operations, services, and programs; to understand the quantitative and qualitative characteristics of inputs, processes, and outputs; and to apply the results from internal evaluations to inform decision making.

To be most effective, internal library evaluations should build on organizational learning that empowers staff by involving them in all stages: from planning through collection to analysis and review to discussion of the results and their implications. This participatory process, along with the installation of the value of the evaluative effort, helps to create a culture of planning, evaluation, and assessment that appreciates the transparency of the library's efforts to provide services as well as to hold itself accountable to all stakeholders.

Exercises

1. Internal library evaluations are most often concerned about the relationships among what three things?

2. Describe library inputs.

3. Describe library processes.

4. Describe library outputs.

5. What is one difference between quantitative and qualitative mechanisms used in internal library evaluation?

6. A user complains about the lack of seating in the library. How might you evaluate this complaint?

7. A user is wondering why an owned yet popular non-reserve book is not on the shelf even though the automated system states it is available. How might you evaluate this question?

8. What type of evaluative study may you undertake to learn if there is a relationship between library usage and library programs?

9. Is user satisfaction an output or an outcome?

10. Users complain about the "long lines" at the circulation desk. What evaluative study may you undertake?

11. How much does it cost to answer a reference question?

12. List five ratios a library may want to use for comparisons with peer or aspirant libraries.

(Answers to these questions are found in the "Appendix" at the back of the book. We encourage different members of a library staff to work on the exercises together and to discuss the results.)

NOTES

1. Sarah M. Pritchard, "Determining Quality in Academic Libraries," *Library Trends* 44, no. 3 (Winter 1996): 574–75.

2. Robert C. Dickeson, *Prioritizing Academic Programs and Services: Reallocating Resources to Achieve Strategic Balance* (San Francisco: Jossey-Bass, 2010).

3. Peter Hernon and Ellen Altman, *Assessing Service Quality: Satisfying the Expectations of Library Customers* (Chicago: American Library Association, 2010).

4. Ray Lyons and Keith Curry Lance, "LJ Index 2012: The Star Libraries," *Library Journal* (November 8, 2012), http://lj.libraryjournal.com/2012/11/industry-news/lj-index-2012-the-star-libraries/.

5

EXTERNAL EVALUATION TO INFORM STAKEHOLDERS AND TO GUIDE CONTINUOUS IMPROVEMENT

xternal evaluation informs stakeholders about how the library adds value to library customers, the parent institution (e.g., the municipality or county, the college or university), and the general community. Because the focus is broader than internal organizational evaluations, external evaluations require the appreciation and understanding of the needs and expectations of key stakeholders based on their perspectives or as individuals or groups sharing common characteristics such as being parents, employers, or students.

Libraries do not operate as stand-alone entities other than in rare instances such as several athenaeums in the United States. As organizations operating within larger institutions, libraries are increasingly expected to document their efficiency and effectiveness while meeting stakeholder expectations and demonstrating the value of library contributions to the success of the institution in achieving its mission and goals. Library accountability instills stakeholder confidence in library operations while building and ensuring ongoing trust and a positive dialogue.

Results from external evaluations, when conveyed in reports, inform stakeholders about how well the library meets the needs and expectations of constituent groups and other stakeholders while aligning services and programs with the institution's mission and goals. Additionally, external evaluation studies may also identify and examine influential factors that are outside the library's managerial controls, such as inflation or the changing demographics of its service population. In turn, evaluative data, analysis, and results inform the library's short- and long-term planning as an input, as well as the library's immediate decision making.

The goal is to create learning organizations in which the workforce functions as a group and everyone continually enhances their capabilities to create programs, services, and activities that contribute to the achievement of the institutional mission and work toward the realization of an organizational vision. Learning organizations focus on the accomplishment of a strategic plan and strategic initiatives, and as such they operate within a culture of evaluation and assessment and use of the data gathered for continuous quality improvement. This chapter provides an overview setting the stage for the next four chapters.

Considering "What" and "How" to Evaluate

An external evaluation study is carried out for the following reasons, ones that are not mutually exclusive. First, the library wants to learn and demonstrate how its services impact users as individuals, support and contribute to the institution's mission by adding value, and benefit the general community it services. Bonnie Gratch Lindauer differentiates between outcomes and impacts. An outcome describes the realized goals of stakeholders whereas an impact describes the direct and indirect effects the library has on users in the aggregate and institution and the community as nonperson entities.[1] Second, as with the results of an internal evaluation, the library wants to plan and implement changes by applying study findings to improve programs, services, management, and resources on behalf of customers, the institution, and the community.

The library's mission should align with its institution's stated mission; a sought-after result from an external evaluation demonstrates that library resources, services, and programs support the institutional mission. To help organize and study the alignment of the library with the institution, a simple four-column grid can be constructed relating the library's goals and objectives to the institution's mission and to the evidence identified to demonstrate impacts and outcomes:

- The goals and objectives from the library's strategic plan identify what the library is doing;
- Identification and explanation of how each of the library's goals and objectives aligns and supports the institution's mission;
- The available evidence identifies the sources of data that are routinely collected to show the status of meeting the objective; and
- That evidence identifies the data yet to be collected. The grid should also identify the data sources, who will collect the evidence, and when they will collect it.

As discussed in chapter 2, evidence-based practice is an ideal application to undertake external evaluations. This evaluation process helps to collect evidence and produce the data necessary for library administrators to analyze and assess impacts and outcomes, apply the findings to implement improvements as part of the organization's planning process, and share the findings and the improvement plan with interested stakeholders. A library with a strong culture of evaluation and assessment will have identified the questions concerning impacts and outcomes, as well as possible actions to take before undertaking the external evaluation.[2]

If one asked different librarians about what services, programs, and resources would be viable areas for external evaluation studies, each one would probably give a different response. Those areas might encompass quality, administration and management, partnerships, customer satisfaction, supporting education, and reputation. Thus, it is important to make decisions based on their alignment with local strategic initiatives.

Quality

Two perspectives are evident when libraries undertake external evaluations to inform stakeholders about matters of quality: that of the library and that of the customer. Quality is difficult to define because the answer must be framed within a local context. For example, a library is likely to define quality different from how a customer or stakeholder would. For purposes of this chapter, quality is the value the library adds to the institution or broader organization and the perceived value that a customer, groups of customers, and others interested in the library receive. Quality is often discussed in contexts such as:

Resources provided to, and used by, the library to enable access and availability to materials. The quality of the program inputs and processes to the library when applied to its infrastructure (collections, personnel, technologies, and facilities) makes significant differences in attaining and sustaining quality.

Services and programming. Quality includes examples of exemplary performance that result in both impact and outcomes. Circulation services provide access and availability on a shared basis through reserve and the general circulation of items that an individual may not be able to borrow elsewhere or afford to purchase, such as laptops, e-reader devices, and scientific calculators. Summer reading programs may increase reading levels for a group of customers, measurable by pre- and post-testing. Free community art displays may bring attention to a local artist resulting in a life-changing outcome for the individual and financial gain for the artist.

Proxies used in peer benchmarking. Oftentimes libraries use comparative peer benchmarking measures as a proxy for quality. For example, how do specific characteristics of the library staff compare with those of peer libraries?

LIBRARY'S PERSPECTIVE

External evaluation studies from the library's perspective are perhaps more numerous as the library uses the results to tell its story about how it adds value to the lives of its service population while supporting the institutional mission. It can do so as part of evaluative studies by relating important output metrics as proxies for quality such as those covered in box 5.1.

Box 5.1

Outputs as Proxies for Quality

**Demographics and Use; Align the Changes in Demographics
to Changes in Library Use**

- the changing demographics of users over time, including age and gender
- the proportion of the community using the library, and more specifically, the percentage of the population who borrowed from the library, down-loaded materials from the library, used the physical collection, and used the virtual collections
- discovering why the user visited the library (e.g., to borrow books or use a workstation to access the Internet)
- who accompanied the user (e.g., peer, child) or person was alone

Collection's Strengths Supporting Needs

- the significance and currency of the holdings, such as the age of the collection (e.g., astronomy books from the 1950s are not relevant unless it is a history of astronomy or science collection)
- relevancy of holdings to the varied needs of its users, such as the inclusion of differing viewpoints and perspectives
- impact of weeding on collection quality (a worthy focus for an external evaluative study; stakeholders are always concerned when books are discarded and may not understand the rationale for collection mainte-nance)
- calculated conspectus factor (used primarily by academic libraries)

**Support for Academic Program Reviews and Accreditations
(Academic Libraries)**

- collection evaluation study becomes part of the external report
- academic libraries may also contribute content and analysis for depart-mental program reviews, most often with information about the align-ment of the library's inputs and outputs to the academic program under review

Library Personnel and Attributes Contributing to Staff Quality

- the profiles and number of staff
- the degrees held by staff
- years of staff experience
- ratio of part-time to full-time staff
- recognitions and awards

(Cont.)

Box 5.1 **Outputs as Proxies for Quality** (Cont.)

- number and type of scholarly contributions (e.g., articles in peer-reviewed journals)
- the number of opportunities for, and the realization of, staff development

Library Deployed Technologies

- the currency of the equipment deployed
- provision of networking technologies to enable users to remotely access and use information materials and other resources 24/7, making it convenient to use the library without physically visiting the facility only during its open hours
- the alignment of the technology with needs; for example, users may no longer need 8mm film projectors

Library Facilities

- adequate number of seats, and type of seating that users will use
- availability of electrical jacks for users
- signage used to navigate users through the building

Services Provided to Support User Needs

- number of hours actually open, days of week and times of day
- hours open when users need them (e.g., open at night to accommodate those who work during the day)
- number of users entering the library, and by day of week and time of day
- number of hours the reference desk is staffed by professional librarians, an example of service delivery supported by librarian expertise
- cost to answer a reference question
- accuracy level of reference questions answered
- level of interlibrary loan transactions, fill rates, and turnaround times to meet the information needs of users even if the sought-after item is not in the local collection. Best practices include an increasing fill rate and decreasing turnaround time.
- circulation transactions by format of materials, and by demographics if possible
- database usage by demographics, days of week and times of day, and from inside the library or remote access (resources available when the library is not open)

Uniqueness of Services and Programs Offered That Align with Community Needs and Are Not Provided Elsewhere (Examples)

- the provision and use of a learning commons
- special collections services that are directly related to specific community needs, including preserving historic artifacts, conducting and preserving oral histories, digitizing local records and items to increase accessibility and availability, and acquiring and managing monographs specifically relevant to the community as part of its historic and cultural record
- an instruction area for teaching computer skills
- a meeting room used for library and nonlibrary activities
- provision and use of specific programs, such as the use of a collection of materials focused on supporting local businesses or public wall displays of local artists
- attendance at programs, such as children's story hours, author readings, and art displays

CUSTOMERS' PERSPECTIVE

The library should also evaluate quality from the customers' perspective. This is most often accomplished by collecting evidence directly from customers about how the library adds value to their lives; in other words, the library needs to learn what customers received from the library's services, and what the customer accomplishes as a result. This concept of value—one focused on the impact of library services—is often referred to as *value as results* or *value in use*. This values concept equates value with the subsequent results from customer interaction with the library and the perceived worth or benefits on how library services help them change in some way. With many methods of collecting evidence available (e.g., focus group interviews and surveys), librarians can elicit information from customers about what the library enables them to do.

A frequently used mechanism, in addition to conducting user surveys, is to calculate an economic value of customer perceptions of their library use, which is then communicated to stakeholders as a proxy for quality. Nearly all stakeholders have a financial perspective; it may be more meaningful for them to be informed about the value of library usage in a financial context as a proxy for quality rather than reviewing tables of output metrics such as the number of articles downloaded from databases. There are two general methodologies to calculate this economic value indicator. One is to learn directly from customers how they value library services in terms of a dollar value, while the second is for the library to calculate an economic value of services on behalf of the customer.

Return on investment (ROI) is utilized to determine a financial amount expressing the importance of library services to individuals within the community. A library saves customers' money by acquiring information resources on their behalf. For example, they may borrow, read, and later return a recreational book for other people to use. The price is such that they could buy the book, but would rather use the library's copy and save their personal funds. In another example, customers may use a library resource that they may not be able to afford to purchase or use a resource that is not available for purchase (e.g., a loose-leaf taxation service) by individuals.

A number of ROI studies have been prepared for public libraries in the past few years. Some of them cover an individual library whereas others address a library with branches, a group of libraries, or all public libraries in a state. The majority of studies report a benefit/cost ratio in the range of $4.00 to $6.00 of benefits for every dollar of the library's budget.[3] The LibValue Project, http://libvalue.cci.utk.edu, provides tools and literature, produced by Carol Tenopir and others, for academic libraries to use in determining ROI. One of the reports is the Scholarly Reading and the Value of Library project, which measures the value and results from access to scholarly publications in six universities in the United Kingdom since 1977.

Administration and Management

Libraries engage in continuous planning to inform resource allocation and to demonstrate to the institution and stakeholders how the library contributes to realizing the goals of the institutional mission as well as to the community as a whole in an efficient and effective manner. An area of library administrators' focus when conducting external evaluation studies is financial value. This perspective recognizes that many stakeholders are interested in the business-like characteristics of library operations, underscoring a popularly held concept that financial management is the means to achieve other goals. Stakeholders with a business perspective expect librarians to demonstrate that they manage their financial resources well (stewardship) and help bring money into their institutions.

An area of financial management to consider for an external evaluation study is the alignment of expenditures to measurable objectives in the library's strategic plan. The input resources applied should directly support measurable output/outcome objectives found in the library's annual operating or budgeting plan, which supports the library's overall strategic plan. For example, if the library stated in its budget plan that it would acquire 1,000 new titles, did it meet that objective by applying sufficient funds to acquire those titles? To relate this objective to quality, we might ask: "Did the acquisition of the titles support the plan to strengthen the collection through ongoing development to support locally identified needs?"

Two commonly used external evaluations involve the library's efficiency and effectiveness. Efficiency involves inputs and outputs; the more outputs the library produces for the same inputs (e.g., personnel and resources), the more efficient the library is operating. Examples of external evaluation studies in efficiency include:

- Ensuring that the duplication of content in a multiplicity of formats is minimized. For example, there is a rationale for having the same content (e.g., a journal title subscription in both print and an electronic version) in two or more sources (e.g., direct subscription or in an aggregated database).
- Staffing. Is the library appropriately staffed when usage is high versus staffing levels based on staff work preferences?
- Cost-benefit analysis which seeks to establish whether the benefits of an investment outweigh the costs. Examples of cost-benefit analysis include decisions concerning outsourcing throughputs, such as outsourcing or keeping technical services in-house, and owning versus leasing of technology that is often replaced. Many libraries will face a cost-benefit analysis over the next ten years to evaluate whether to replace their existing integrated library system with an open-source alternative whose development is shared by other libraries worldwide.

Library effectiveness relates how well the library, as an organization, fulfills its stated goals and objectives:

- Do the services provided meet their measurable objectives?
- Is the library appropriately communicating with its customers and other stakeholders, ensuring the messaging and content use the correct communication channel and the proper language to reduce or eliminate the noise?
- Is the library a partner that collaborates and advocates with other organizations to accomplish its customer- and community-based goals and objectives?

An effective library produces the expected or intended result by relating inputs and throughputs with the intended outcomes. Although effectiveness is often evaluated from the customers' perspective, it may also be evaluated from the library and institution's perspective.

A library may also want to demonstrate to external stakeholders how efficiencies lead to effectiveness. For example, as the library increases the quantity of materials it acquires through consortia, it realizes increased fund savings from economies of scale. The savings can be applied to acquire additional information content. The acquired content may, therefore, improve library effectiveness as the accessibility and availability of content through efficiency create a positive outcome for users.

Increasingly, stakeholders are asking about the revenue generated by the library to support its services and programs goals. The library may focus an evaluation study on the revenue generated by grants or gift funds or on revenue generated from fees or by other means that help offset some or all of the program expenses. Another focus can be the degree to which the library has cultivated external relationships with corporations, economic development agencies, joint ventures or other outreach efforts that produced revenue, the donation of equipment, or the receipt of in-kind services.

Another area of evaluation for administration and management examines external factors over which the library has little to no control. Examples include changes in the service area's demographics and economic conditions. Examining these issues may reveal a cyclical trend. For example, deteriorating regional or national economic conditions impacting the personal finances of community residents may result in increased use of the library as well as changing needs or demands for services and programs, such as information about career changes. Additionally, weakening economic conditions locally may directly affect the library, reducing its expected revenue amounts. A localized change in economic conditions, such as the relocation of a major area employer elsewhere, will impact the library, its revenue, and its services and programs.

Library management may also demonstrate economic returns to the resources that the institution or broader organization invests in the library. An institutional return on investment is similar to that developed by the library on behalf of customers. For an institutional ROI, the library may use all of the services calculated for customers but add other tangibles, including the gate counts and the estimated value of the general collection as an asset versus the estimated value of the collection's usage the past year. The dollar sum calculated for usage and assets is compared to the dollar amount of the institutional investment:

> institutional return on investment = summed valuation of usage and assets divided by the amount of the institutional investment (budget allocation).

The results of this study can be stated in terms of a ratio: "for each dollar invested in the library, the library returned $N.NN to the institution in services provided and assets managed." An example includes the public libraries in the state of Florida, which, in 2008, returned $8.32 for $1.00 invested from all sources.[4]

In addition to ROI evaluative studies, public libraries have evaluated their community impact using another economic activity. The multiplier effects result from the trickle-down effect of spending in an economy and demonstrating the library's impact on employment and the local, regional, and national economy. These effects can include library employee salaries, library purchases of materials which benefit vendors, and the salaries of vendor employees, all of which grow economies. Other elements of multiplier effects include visitors and relocations. As an example, the total revenue investment in Florida's public libraries was $661.5 million in 2008. Based on an analysis of what would happen if public libraries ceased to exist, the total economic return attributable to the existence of Florida public libraries was $6.23 billion.[5]

An economic study conducted for the Free Library in Philadelphia found that homes located within a quarter of a mile of a library were worth, on average, $9,630 more than homes more than a quarter of a mile from a library. For homes between a quarter of a mile and half a mile from a library, the additional value was $650. Libraries were responsible in 2009 for $698 million in home values in Philadelphia. The additional home values generated by proximity to a library produced an additional $18.5 million in property taxes to the city and school district each year.[6]

Another means to demonstrate effective library administration to stakeholders is through financial stewardship. The library submits a budget for review that requests adequate resources to meet the reasonable expectations of library users when balanced against other institutional needs. Once the budget is approved and allocated, the library expends its resources effectively to support the library's strategic directions and mission. Additionally, effective stewardship increases the accuracy of expenditures, producing few, if any, errors and passes all financial audits. Libraries demonstrating effective stewardship expend their allocations as appropriate, not diverting funds away from approved and expected objectives and outputs toward unapproved or unnecessary projects.

In addition to economic impact, libraries can demonstrate their social impact as well. Social impact can be defined in different ways, but in the context of library services it may be thought of as any effect of a service (or other event) on an individual or group. In one public library study, respondents stated that the following were the most important reasons for using limited public funds on libraries:

- Libraries help individuals and companies solve problems;
- Libraries offer individuals enjoyment via leisure time reading;
- Libraries proliferate knowledge which everyone should know; and
- Libraries promote democracy.[7]

Another outcome, social inclusion, can be defined as mutual respect and communication between groups and individuals where everyone has equal access to opportunities. Libraries strive toward social inclusion by creating an environment and services that cater to people who normally do not use the library, particularly those who are marginalized and socially excluded, such as youth, the homeless, and the unemployed. In the areas of social capital and community building, studies reveal that the community-building potential of libraries stems from their provision of an open learning environment and a safe, nondiscriminatory, free and accessible place, partnerships with other community organizations, and encouragement of self-reliance or helping people to do things for themselves. Evaluating the library's social impact can provide strong evidence of the library's contribution to the institution's goals and the good of the broader community.

Partnerships

Stakeholders are increasingly interested in the partnerships in which libraries develop and participate. There are two distinct spheres of library partnerships: intra-institutional and external-institutional. Intra-institutional partnerships are those that exist between the library and other organizational members of the institution to provide services and programs to shared users or constituents. A study of this type of partnership evaluates the number, scope, and outcomes of partnerships between faculty and librarians at any level in K 12 and beyond; stakeholders are interested in evaluation studies that demonstrate how the collaborative efforts between the library and the faculty create a positive learning outcome for students. With some exceptions, librarians at any educational level depend on teachers for instructional access to students. Partnerships between librarians and teachers occur in three forms: cooperation, coordination, and collaboration. In some cases, librarians and teachers cooperate by communicating informally about student assignments, but work independently to support students. Other librarians and teachers coordinate their work by meeting together to discuss student learning, but set goals separately, plan learning experiences separately, and teach and assess separately. Collaboration occurs when teachers and librarians jointly set goals, design learning experiences, teach, and evaluate student studies.[8]

Another evaluative study may explore the number of committees on which librarians serve as members and the impact those committees have at the institutional level. Other partnerships may involve local organizations in an effort to realize mutual benefits, including broadening services or advocacy. An example would be the provision of career counselors from a local government's economic development agency to conduct programs or otherwise counsel citizens in library space.

External-institutional partnerships occur for a variety of reasons. Libraries of all types share resources and may partner with libraries of other institutions to realize shared goals by forming or joining a consortium or some other arrangement in an effort to manage funds effectively through economies of scale. Examples of evaluative studies include:

- economies of scale to acquire access to e-book and e-journal databases which the local library cannot afford to subscribe to or license on its own;
- materials borrowing and lending through interlibrary agreements which may involve an area or state library-to-library courier service;
- technologies such as a consortium sharing the acquisition and operating costs of an integrated library system; and
- leveraging operational costs through regional or statewide contracts to purchase supplies.

These partnerships may be informal member service organizations (i.e., a library agrees to lend materials to other libraries without charging transaction fees) while a second type of agreement is based on formal governance arrangements in which each member library as a voting member may direct financial or other resources for the good of the library and the consortium's membership may acquire or provide specific services.

Another type of partnership may go so far as to jointly share physical facilities as well as specific service responsibilities on behalf of the users of two institutions (e.g., a shared public and academic library facility). External evaluation studies would include:

- discovering the tangible benefits received by each library through the financial savings through economies of scale;
- cost savings by sharing operational costs (e.g., the difference in costs necessary to acquire and maintain a local integrated library system versus sharing one with one or more libraries); and
- the outcomes as perceived by the library and its users from access to shared services.

Many public libraries maintain an information and referral clearinghouse about regional service providers as well as work directly with other agencies to support services, such as establishing lending libraries and conducting library programming at nursing homes. An example of an evaluative study is the number and scope of these partnerships; outcomes provide narratives and other examples about the impact of these partnerships on the respective clientele.

Higher education has a distinct recognition for the value of partnerships. Institutions may be recognized for their external impacts through their attainment of the Carnegie Foundation's Community Engagement Classification, which describes the collaboration between institutions of higher education and their larger communities (local, regional/state, national, global) for the mutually beneficial exchange of knowledge and resources in a context of partnership and reciprocity.[9] Academic libraries and their external partnerships may help the institution achieve this sought-after external recognition.

Customer Satisfaction

The money and/or time users save as a result of their interaction with the library, from the library's perspective, is often communicated to the external stakeholders to demonstrate the library's value. However, librarians must learn from customers how they value the library from their perspective. Customer satisfaction has external evaluative applications in addition to its importance in internal evaluative studies.

Examining satisfaction from an external perspective helps the library discover and understand the needed and unnecessary characteristics of its programs and services. In fact, expressions concerning levels of satisfaction may become a proxy when evaluating aspects of library quality. For example, publicly expressed customer satisfaction for library services, programs, and resources may demonstrate local or regional demand and, as a result of the library externally publicizing the results, create new demand from new-to the library users.

Box 5.2 provides examples of customer satisfaction metrics with the library's infrastructure. Whatever data are collected should be used to improve library services and the customer experience. Satisfaction can also be related to retention, persistence, and completion, which are terms most often associated with higher education. However, retention and persistence can be extrapolated to all types of libraries as proxies

Box 5.2
Customer Satisfaction

With Library Resources (Customers Find the Library Resources They Need)

- number of written complaints and compliments submitted by users
- customers can access collections from all user locations (e.g., branch libraries, off-site remote access)

With Technologies

- customers choose libraries' web interface as their starting point
- customers characterize the libraries' interface as intuitive
- customers judge the libraries' interface as a reason for their success

With the Facilities (e.g., Seats, Tables, Physical Layout)

With the Help and Service They Receive from Staff

for users returning to a library because services and programs are delivered with consistency and continuity over time by a quality infrastructure with satisfied customers as an outcome. Completion, more commonly referred to as graduation, is a proxy for following through and delivering (finishing) what was promised.

Supporting Education

Most, if not all, libraries support individual or group education. A long-standing mission of many public libraries includes informing the public as a whole and serving as a source for encouraging and facilitating lifelong personal education. Public libraries support individual improvement by creating a reading culture through literacy and information competence, instilling the value of appreciating lifelong learning, and helping individuals develop and acquire skills, competencies, tools, processes, and values. The wider effects include benefits to the society's economic, political, and social well-being attributable to greater employment levels; increased participation in democratic activities; and an improved quality of life by generating capacity for community members to share resources and develop a sense of belonging.

An important library customer group is students. Libraries may not explicitly address how their resources and services make a qualitative difference to student learning, staff development, and faculty scholarship.[10] External evaluation studies help libraries explain and show stakeholders their contribution to learning. For example, student learning outcomes include values and skills and are supported by school and public libraries as well as academic libraries. Much of the external evaluation results demonstrated by public library users are qualitative and involve stories about how public library resources have positively changed lives. Students attending traditional face-to-face classes as well as online learners, teachers, and other faculty members discover the content to support curriculum-based courses in the many library-based sources supported and funded through state libraries. Libraries also recognize that evaluation helps them identify weaknesses in their instruction and services that can be improved in the continuous effort to support learning and teaching effectively.

Learning and teaching outcomes that libraries are evaluating for external study and reporting include students becoming self-reliant in information literacy skills by:

- identifying information needs;
- finding/locating information;
- selecting relevant information;
- assessing and evaluating information;
- synthesizing;
- using information effectively;
- presenting information;
- understanding and using the information search process;
- understanding different formats of information and dealing with them effectively;
- expanding their use of types of sources;
- being aware (having an accurate mental model) of the structured nature of information;
- understanding how to evaluate bias and the credibility of information;
- appreciating the way the quality of information varies along a historical continuum;

- understanding the social/ethical/political/economic implications of information and intellectual property;
- understanding the research process through which new knowledge is created;
- understanding the scholarly communications cycle and its application to scholarly research;
- becoming self-confident and comfortable in information-rich environments;
- developing attitudes of openness, flexibility, curiosity, creativity, and an appreciation of the value of a broad perspective;
- preparing to become lifelong learners able to identify, access, and use effectively a variety of information resources;
- transferring the skills learned to support other information needs;
- becoming proficient with appropriate information technologies; and
- becoming able to evaluate and apply information to meet academic, personal, and desired workforce readiness skills identified by employers.[11]

Increasingly, regional and program accreditation efforts in higher education involve external reviewers interested in student learning outcomes and other measures by which the institution, academic programs, and library impact students. Results from academic libraries' evaluation studies of learning and teaching are often a mixture of quantitative and qualitative, with several proxies substituting for direct causations.

Academic libraries often instruct students in classroom settings inside or outside the library. The library may conduct assessments before, during, and after an instruction to receive student feedback concerning the effectiveness of the instruction and the perceived relevancy of the instruction content. Library learning assessments should be authentic, integrated performance assessments focused on identified institutional and program learning outcomes related to information literacy. Librarians may also keep track of the requests that instruction generates; for example, a student having attended an instruction may call, e-mail, or conduct a face-to-face consultation with a librarian as a follow-up to the instruction. Additionally, the library wants to discover if the student grasped the objective for the instruction: the stated learning outcome. Examples for evaluative studies include:

- positive measured change in skills;
- student learning outcomes;
- students engage with librarians to support course work;
- students articulate libraries' contribution to their learning;
- student scores on information literacy tests; and
- students evaluate information literacy classes as effective.

Librarians are also interested in faculty perceptions of the library's contribution to learning. External evaluative studies concerning library instruction include the number of repeat faculty requestors for instruction versus new requestors. Repeat requests by faculty for instruction may indicate sustained interest because faculty note student learning gains as a result of their interactions with library instruction and library resources. New requests may indicate that the library is making inroads with faculty concerning the effectiveness of time spent in library instruction sessions and with library resources. Librarians also collaborate with faculty regarding ways to incorporate library collections and services into effective education experiences for students. The number and scope of faculty/librarian instructional collaborations concerning curriculum, assignments, projects, or assessment design, along with the measured integration of library resources and services into course syllabi, websites, lectures, laboratories, texts, reserve readings, and co-curricular activities, are other fertile areas for evaluation. The results from these evaluations are important to convey to institutional stakeholders. Examples of evaluative studies include:

- the number of faculty requests to create customized online course guides;
- the extent of use of the guides, subject guides, or tutorials prepared by library staff;
- the number of library-to-faculty collaborations of the information literacy program;
- the extent to which faculty value librarians as collaborators;
- the extent to which faculty include information literacy outcomes on their syllabi;
- the extent to which faculty evaluate literacy outcomes skills as a result of contact with librarians; and
- the extent to which faculty participate in and value workshops provided by librarians.

Academic libraries evaluate their support of faculty research, scholarly productivity, and professional development. A qualitative metric is faculty acknowledgment in written communications or otherwise published of library support for providing access to or securing information resources via interlibrary loan they deemed essential to support their work on publications, patents, research-generated products, and technology transfer. Quantitative metrics indicate the number of library resources used by the faculty in their work as well as the number of products produced. Librarians also provide direct and indirect assistance to the faculty and researchers when they submit proposals to request financial assistance through grants. Quantitative evaluative metrics include the number of grant proposals submitted (funded or unfunded) and the value of grants funded. Other qualitative and quantitative evaluative metrics include the number of resources on the scholarship of teaching and learning requested by faculty and acquired by the library, the number of tenure/promotion judgments on which supportive information was requested from librarians (e.g., the number of citations from peer-reviewed journals), and the number of faculty recruitment/search committees with librarians as members.

Higher education uses several surrogates to evaluate students, including:

- student success, including internship success, job placement, job salaries, feedback from employers, and professional/graduate school acceptance;
- student achievement, including course completions, grade point average (GPA), professional/educational test scores such as the Graduate Record Examination (GRE), Medical College Admission Test (MCAT), Law School Admission Test (LSAT), Collegiate Assessment of Academic Proficiency (CAAP), Collegiate Learning Assessment (CLA), Measure of Academic Proficiency and Progress (MAPP), and licensure tests;
- student experience, attitude, and perception of quality, including self-report engagement studies (e.g., National Survey of Student Engagement), senior/alumni studies, and alumni donations.

Academic libraries, for instance, may conduct an evaluative study to learn if students who use their resources have higher GPAs than average, and if students who work in the libraries have higher than average GPAs. However, given grade inflation, such a study may not produce meaningful results.

A means for tracking educational outcomes is an assessment management system, which can be developed by individual libraries or institutions, or purchased through third-parties (e,g., WeaveONLINE, TracDat, eLumen, ILAT, Blackboard Learn's assessment module, LiveText, Tk20). These systems help higher education librarians and educators manage learning outcomes assessment by recording and maintaining data on each outcome, facilitating connections to similar outcomes throughout an institution, and generating reports documenting progress in meeting strategic or organizational goals. They are most effective when deployed on an institution-wide basis enabling higher education institutions to link outcomes vertically (within units) and horizontally (across divisions, colleges, departments, programs, and libraries). In this way, assessment management systems recognize that students do not gain knowledge, skills, or abilities from just one course, just in their major, or just in the classroom; rather they enable institutions to capture evidence of student learning through all their interactions with institutional units.[12]

Reputation

Reputation, as a possible result from external evaluation studies, is often viewed as a proxy for validation of quality. Libraries can attain their own reputation as well as contribute to their institution's reputation by providing a service or collection which is unique or distinctive, by bringing beneficial recognition to it and the institution through winning an award, or through peer comparisons.

It may be that the most common source of reputation is through comparisons and analysis of quantitative metrics with one's peers. On the public library side, the *LJ* Index of Public Library Service (LJI) compares U.S. public libraries on the quantities of services they deliver: how quantities of selected services provided by a library compare with libraries within its peer group. The LJI scores are based on four per capita service output statistics (library visits, circulation, program attendance, and public Internet computer use), which are closely related statistically. For each library, each of the four output statistics is measured against the average for the library's peer group. A high value on one or more statistics can compensate for lower values on other statistics. This "sensitivity" of the index as explained by its authors "is intended to encourage both the identification of excellence in specific services as well as thoughtful review of the validity and reliability of local data reports." The LJI authors state that these specific service outputs do not reflect quality, excellence, effectiveness, or value of services to the library's community, nor do they indicate whether library service output levels are appropriate for the library's community, nor the extent to which services sufficiently address community needs.[13] Despite these stated limitations, the LJI as structured in peer comparison groups and with the awarding of three to five stars is a ranking system that serves as an instrument for external local reputation.

Each year the Association of Research Libraries calculates the Library Investment Index as a summary of relative size among the university library members. The metrics are total library expenditures, salaries and wages of professional staff, total library materials expenditures, and total number of professional and support staff. The index is not an effort to measure a library's services, quality of collections, or success in meeting the needs of users.[14] Because the resultant index is used to align the libraries in a table from the highest to lowest ranking, it is a de facto source of external reputation among the association's membership.

Reputation is also created by providing unique or respected services that are externally acknowledged or otherwise recognized. Higher education institutional reputation includes faculty scholarship and research outcomes. Scholarly impact includes citation counts (counting the number of times articles are cited by other writings) and usage data (number of times a digital article has been downloaded, as well as who is downloading the article). Faculty research productivity includes the number of publications, patents, research-generated products, and grants submitted. Research outcomes include the level of research and development expenditures, doctorate degrees awarded each year, post-doctoral appointments, research awards per year, faculty membership in prestigious academies, and faculty quality rankings.

Academic libraries contribute to institutional reputation. The library may fund or otherwise manage an institutional repository which increases access and availability of internally produced information, helping to build external reputation and prestige. Evaluative measures include the number of faculty contributing to the institutional repository. Academic librarians may also enhance institutional and library reputation through their scholarly contributions to the LIS literature.[15]

Sharon Weiner, who conducted the major study of academic library reputation, examined more than 200 doctoral universities and assorted cross-institutional performance indicators. Using performance variables representing the institutional level (grants; instruction, research, and student services expenditures; and alumni, foundation, and corporate giving) and the library level (library expenditures, reference transactions, library presentation, attendees at library presentations, and library professional staff), library expenditures was the only consistently significant variable, but the results indicate that libraries contribute to institutional reputation.[16] Still, the types of metrics covered in this chapter should not be ignored as the concept of reputation is becoming more complex.

Public libraries contribute to the reputation of their parent institution as well as their geopolitical unit (e.g., town, city, or county). Reputation is often recognized through the public's satisfaction as analyzed via surveys, voter approval for tax or budget increases or bonding for building construction, LJI star rating for community engagement with other service providers, and the advocacy of library principles such as resisting local efforts to censor access and availability of information in a multiplicity of formats. Gauging the community's awareness of the library's services and programs (market penetration) is a useful evaluation study.

Other sources of reputation are the unique collections and services supported and provided by the library. Unique collections are oftentimes focused on the locality and region with content inclusive of print and oral histories, genealogy, maps, photographs, and local newspapers. Reputation may be linked to these unique collections as well as the conversion of special collection items into digital formats, increasing accessibility for remote access. Collections may also be established for local authors or celebrated residents, or be focused on a person or family and include their public work as well as their correspondence, or a literature genre such as science fiction. External evaluative studies could include counts of all of these unique collections and their use, the percentage of collections converted to digital formats to increase access, and the external awareness of unique content.

Reputation may also be evaluated by examining unique programs and services, and how they support the needs of the locality and region, as well as institutional goals. Locally inspired programming may include children story hours, poetry readings, and art displays. Services may include specialized instruction such as intergenerational computer literacy and use of technology; tax preparation sessions; résumé writing and job-seeking assistance; and the provision of spaces such as providing access to a meeting room for nonlibrary activities. Other contributions to reputation include community engagement though partnerships, library staff contributing to scholarship and practice through conferences and the professional literature, and recognition through awards. External evaluation studies explore narratives about how these unique services and programs affect peoples' lives, and produce external-to-the-library publicity.

Concluding Thoughts

This chapter identified several evaluative areas: quality, library administration and management, partnerships, customer satisfaction, education support, and reputation. Certainly other organizational areas can be identified and evaluated based upon the localized context and mission of the institution. External evaluation studies should include their research and implementation designs along with the analysis and results. If possible, the library should make its design and results widely available through a website or in the professional literature, enabling other libraries to replicate the process. Widespread usage of evaluation designs and results may become a best practice or be incorporated into a library association's standards and guidelines.

Libraries want to play a transformational role in the lives of their users. Librarians are increasingly called on to demonstrate how the library adds value by providing evidence in understandable ways to a multiplicity of interested stakeholders about customer outcomes from their interactions with the library; contributions to the success of the institution's mission, values, and goals; and positive impacts on the greater good of the broader community. External evaluation studies seek to learn if a program or service serves individuals and the community in ways that no other program does, determines the quality provided and ultimately recognized, and demonstrates to external audiences how the library supports the institutional mission.

The library accomplishes this by aligning itself with the institutional mission through its organizational planning and the handling of daily operations. External evaluation studies are systematically undertaken to collect, analyze, and convey the evidence from its operations, thereby demonstrating the library's accountability to various stakeholders. The evaluative data are subsequently applied to ongoing planning and operations in the effort to improve continuously.

A common thread is that external evaluations must have relevancy and be of interest to external stakeholders. If the evaluation is of interest only to the library, it is more likely to be an internal evaluation and its application organizational-based rather than institutional- or community-based. However, it is also important that a wide range of external evaluation studies be undertaken because of the varied interests of the stakeholders. Many stakeholders will want to review evaluations that demonstrate the library's financial health. While costs and usage do not indicate *how well* the library is doing, input, process, and output metrics are important to groups of stakeholders and should not be shunned because they do not demonstrate an impact on individuals or groups. However, libraries should not depend on input and output financial measures as their only indicators of contributing to the well-being of users, the institution, and the community. Data from external evaluations can also be judiciously applied for comparison with a library's peers. There are many sources for comparative data from national surveys conducted by governments and associations. Comparative applicability, however, has limitations due to different institutional missions.

Exercises

1. Why would a library conduct an evaluation for external use?

2. What are viable areas for external evaluation studies?

3. Outputs are often used by libraries as proxies for quality. List at least one output for each component of a library's infrastructure that has been used as a proxy for quality, and two for services provided.

4. What would be a simple way to express a value to interested stakeholders of users borrowing books (monographs)?

5. Briefly explain the importance of evaluating a library's economies of scale.

6. Identify at least one external pressure that libraries have no control over, but must deal with when evaluating operations.

7. What services would a library consider from its perspective when calculating a return on investment?

8. The multiplier effect involving libraries has been measured in several states. What do you think is the biggest multiplier factor as contributed by the library?

9. What factors may a librarian evaluate concerning library and faculty/teacher partnerships?

10. What are some of the input and output measures that a library would consider providing to stakeholders to highlight its reputation, especially in comparison with its peer libraries?

(Answers to these questions are in the "Appendix" at the back of the book. We encourage different members of a library staff to work on the exercises together and to discuss the results.)

NOTES

1. Bonnie Gratch Lindauer, "Defining and Measuring the Library's Impact on Campuswide Outcomes," *College & Research Libraries* 59, no. 6 (November 1998): 550.

2. Christine Urquhart, "How Do I Measure the Impact of My Service?" in *Evidence-Based Practice for Information Professionals: A Handbook*, ed. Andrew Booth and Anne Brice (London: Facet, 2004), 212.

3. See Joseph R. Matthews, "What's the Return on ROI? The Benefits and Challenges of Calculating Your Library's Return on Investment," *Library Leadership and Management* 25, no. 1 (2011): 1–14.

4. University of West Florida, Haas Center for Business Research and Economic Development, "Taxpayer Return on Investment in Florida Public Libraries" (May 2010), 3, http://haas.uwf.edu/library/library _study/DraftFinal.pdf.

5. Ibid.

6. University of Pennsylvania, Fels Institute of Government, Fels Research & Consulting, *The Economic Value of the Free Library in Philadelphia* (October 21, 2010), 5, www.freelibrary.org/about/Fels_Report.pdf.

7. Association of College and Research Libraries, *Value of Academic Libraries: A Comprehensive Research Review and Report*, prepared by Megan Oakleaf (Chicago: Association of College and Research Libraries, 2010), 80.

8. Ibid., 58.

9. Carnegie Foundation for the Advancement of Teaching, "Classification Description: Community Engagement Elective Classification," http://classifications.carnegiefoundation.org/descriptions/community _engagement.php.

10. Lindauer, "Defining and Measuring the Library's Impact on Campuswide Outcomes," 547.

11. Ibid., 564.

12. Association of College and Research Libraries, *Value of Academic Libraries*, 12, 45.

13. Ray Lyons and Keith Curry Lance, "America's Star Libraries, 2012: Top-Rated Libraries," *Library Journal* (November 8, 2012), http://lj.libraryjournal.com/2012/11/managing-libraries/lj-index/class-of-2012/americas-star-libraries-2012-top-rated-libraries/; and Ray Lyons and Keith Curry Lance, "The LJ Index: Frequently Asked Questions (FAQ)," *Library Journal* (November 8, 2012), http://lj.libraryjournal.com/stars-faq/ #FAQ1.

14. Association of Research Libraries, "ARL Index" (2012), www.arl.org/stats/index/index.shtml.

15. Thompson Reuters offers ResearcherID, which enables academic institutions, perhaps in conjunction with their libraries, to collect and manage information related to faculty productivity, including gathering cited and citation metrics. The Comparative Data Citation Index, available through the Web of Knowledge, connects digital research, book content, conference proceedings, and journal literature to draw together a wide array of scholarly output to gauge the extent of faculty recognition. It may be that many faculty members do not favor the centralization of such data and the campuswide comparisons that likely emerge.

16. Sharon Weiner, "The Contribution of the Library to the Reputation of a University," *Journal of Academic Librarianship* 35, no. 1 (January 2009): 3–13.

6

MEASURING SATISFACTION

Everyone working in a service industry talks about customer satisfaction; some see it as the "holy grail" of a service industry. There is increased interest in measuring it and in demonstrating customer loyalty. If someone purchases a product or uses a particular service, it is likely that, by snail- or e-mail, or by telephone, that customer will be asked to participate in a short survey about his or her experience and the extent of satisfaction with the product or experience. Anyone making a major purchase such as the purchase of a home might be informed by the salesperson or the team that arranged the purchase that he or she will receive a survey and be asked to mark a score of "extremely satisfied" to every question. If the borrower cannot give such a score someone, perhaps a member of the mortgage team, might ask how they can improve the not-yet-completed experience. In the case of health care, all hospital employees in an organization that measures patient satisfaction are expected to understand the value of the patient as a reflection of the success of the organization. However, interest in patient satisfaction is not of high concern throughout the health care industry. Still, for those organizations insisting that patients come first, both patients and their families appreciate an organization that stands out from its competitors, and they are likely to return and share their experience with others.

Customer satisfaction is the state of mind that customers have about an organization, product, or service when their expectations have been met or exceeded (or conversely not met) over a lifetime of use (*overall service satisfaction*) or their experience in using that organization, product, or service on a particular occasion (*service encounter satisfaction*). Any investigation could focus on either type of customer satisfaction, a concept that leads to loyalty to and reuse of a product, service, or organization. It also leads to recommendations for improved use or purchase by others in the community.

Gaps Model of Service Quality

Customer satisfaction measurement focuses on the gap between customer expectations and performance perceptions. That gap refers to the Gaps Model (or Five Gaps Model) of Service Quality, which posits (see figure 6.1):

Gap 1 as the distance between what customers expect and what managers think they expect.

Gap 2 as the distance between management perception and the actual specification of the customer experience. To examine this gap, managers need to specify the level of service they believe is needed.

Gap 3 as the distance between the customer experience specification and the delivery of the experience. Managers need to monitor the customer experience that their organization delivers in order to make sure it meets the specification.

Gap 4 is the distance between the delivery of the customer experience and what is communicated to customers. Organizations often exaggerate what they will provide to customers, or they discuss the best case rather than the likely case, raising customer expectations and harming customer perceptions.

Gap 5 as the distance between a customer's perception of the experience and the customer's expectation of the service. Those expectations are shaped by word of mouth, personal needs, and past and current experiences.

Typically organizations and researchers have focused on the last gap and managers would like it to be inconsequential. The existence of a gap might also be used to determine customer value, which is defined as the distance between the values the customer gains from owning and using a product and the costs of obtaining the product. This gap might be addressed as part of a study about return on investment.

The Gaps Model encompasses two separate concepts: one is service quality and the other is satisfaction. From the 1980s to the early twenty-first century, service organizations tended to focus on the former and

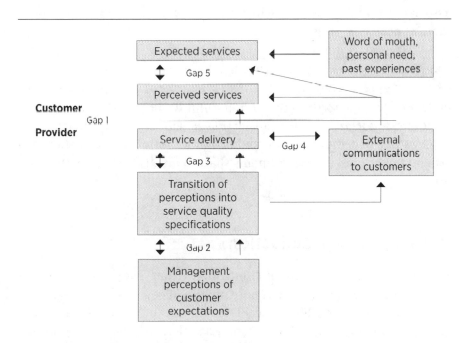

Figure 6.1   The Gaps Model of Service Quality

to make comparisons with similar organizations. In doing so, research focused on statements about customer expectations that, if deemed important to customers, the organization would devote the resources to addressing those statements and thereby elevating the level of customer satisfaction.

Today many stakeholders, such as accreditation organizations (e.g., for academic institutions) and members of boards and Friends' groups (public libraries) expect libraries, among others, to monitor and report on customer satisfaction. They most likely view satisfaction as a reflection of library performance. As libraries position themselves better to provide new services and reconsider present ones, they recognize that an information or knowledge society places a premium on access to information and the ability to use technology. Technology adds value to the library's traditional offerings, and the public, most likely, appreciates public places that encourage them to find, share, interact, reflect, enjoy, and learn. In such an environment, there are increased opportunities for libraries to assume new roles and initiate services not commonly associated with libraries, for which the typical image is of a warehouse of print books.

Satisfaction assumes added importance because libraries operate in a competitive, ever-changing environment. Customers are becoming more demanding, less tolerant, and critical when their expectations are not met. Service organizations find it important to train staff with regard to customer service. Customer satisfaction is something that many businesses strive to achieve in good and bad times. After all, unsatisfied customers might not return and might share their displeasure with many others.

Methods of Data Collection

Figure 6.2 shows different methodologies that enable librarians to gauge customer satisfaction. Those methodologies might be characterized in three ways. First, except for the use of comment cards and possibly complaint/compliment analysis, they involve active means of data collection. Active refers to making an effort to approach and engage customers, whereas passive includes the placement of cards, for instance, throughout the library for interested customers to pick up, complete, and return. Making a comment, either a compliment, complaint, or suggestion, involves a voluntary action on the part of the customer, who initiates an in-person or online interaction with the library. Anyone providing contact information invites, but does not necessarily expect, interaction; in fact, they might be surprised that the organization reaches out and seeks a dialogue. For this reason managers should regard such situations as opportunities to gain loyal supporters.

A digital suggestion box is useful for crisis management, meaning it is better to deal with potential problems as they arise than letting problems fester and ultimately blow up. One technique that some businesses use is to encourage customers to communicate directly with them, perhaps through a Twitter-feed, which provides transparent customer service. Another example is IdeaStorm, a Dell website dedicated to soliciting ideas from its users. On the community site, people post ideas about how to improve the company's products. Clearly, a passive approach in fact might be active, to an extent, if libraries promote it and treat the site as a major means of communication—between customers and library staff as well as among library customers.

Second, the methodologies might invite interaction with customers (surveys and interviews) or ask proxies to visit the library in person or online (mystery shopping), or react to an action initiated by the customer (complaint/compliment analysis, and comment cards). Third, except for

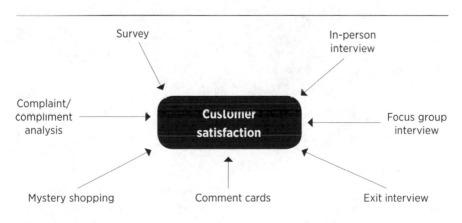

Figure 6.2 Methodologies for Studying Customer Satisfaction

mystery shopping, the methodologies involve customer self-reporting revealing what they want to disclose or think at the moment. People might mistakenly characterize their actions and thinking because they have not really thought about their preferences or how they go about gathering relevant information. They might overtly simplify the process of information-gathering.

When the library staff invites participation, managers must be concerned about the response rate and how well that rate represents everyone eligible for participation. In the case of social networks, it is becoming more evident that people are willing to reveal more about themselves, and their comments might influence others.[1] For this reason, an additional methodology might be content analysis, which involves using text data to create coding categories that enable comparisons across comments and over time.

Instead of presenting each methodology, this chapter focuses on use of a customer survey delivered by e-mail, snail mail, distributed in the library, or offered on a home page. Readers interested in all of the methodologies should consult the sources listed in box 6.1.

Box 6.1
Key Writings

Hernon, Peter, and Ellen Altman. *Assessing Service Quality: Satisfying the Expectations of Library Customers.* Chicago: American Library Association, 2010.

Hernon, Peter, and Joseph R. Matthews, *Listening to the Customer.* Santa Barbara, CA: Libraries Unlimited, 2011.

Hernon, Peter, Robert E. Dugan, and Danuta A. Nitecki. *Engaging in Evaluation and Assessment Research.* Santa Barbara, CA: Libraries Unlimited, 2011.

CUSTOMER SURVEY

In our opinion, Counting Opinions has created a standard satisfaction questionnaire for academic and public libraries. The form, which can be tailored for individual library use, provides questions to determine the extent of the satisfaction gap (gap analysis) and other questions about customer preferences and use patterns. The form might also be available in different versions. The Markham Public Library (Ontario, Canada), for instance, offers the form in the following versions: 2–3 minutes, 5–7 minutes, up to 15 minutes, and a version limited to summer reading programs, http://mpl.countingopinions.com/. Table 6.1 reprints only those questions from the Counting Opinions' form amendable to gap analysis, while box 6.2 shows some other questions that libraries could add if they prefer to create their own form.

Box 6.2
Some Other General Satisfaction Questions

1. Based on your experience in using this library today [or Based on your collective experiences in using this library],

    • what are we doing that you particularly like?
    • what are we doing that you particularly dislike?
    • what do you like *best* about us?
    • what do you like *least* about us?

2. If we could do ONE thing to improve, what should it be?

3. Would you recommend this library to others—friends, colleagues, and acquaintances? [Response options could be yes/no, or a ten-point scale.]

4. Have your recommended this library to others? Yes ___ No___. If you answered "yes," please describe the circumstances.

CONDUCTING THE SURVEY

Peter Hernon and Ellen Altman summarize twenty-nine points to address in conducting a customer satisfaction survey and listening to what customers have to say.[2] The points fall into the following categories: planning, identification of which customers to survey, constructing and asking the questions, generating an acceptable response rate, editing and archiving the data, analyzing the data, and writing the findings for others to read. An additional category might be the investigation of other data collection instruments such as to gauge employee satisfaction. Central to all of the categories is the linkage of the study to a planning process and the use of the evidence gathered to demonstrate accountability and make ongoing service improvements.

Table 6.1

Customer Satisfaction Survey: Selected Questions

Question	1	2	3	4	5	6	7	8	9	10
Overall, how important is this library to you?	<not important ○	○	○	○	○	○	○	○	○	○ very important>
Overall, how satisfied are you with the services of this library?	<not satisfied ○	○	○	○	○	○	○	○	○	○ very satisfied>
How well do these services compare to your expectations?	<fall short ○	○	○	○	○	○	○	○	○	○ exceed>
Overall, how do you rate the quality of these services?	<low quality ○	○	○	○	○	○	○	○	○	○ high quality>
Would you recommend the services of this library to others?	<unlikely ○	○	○	○	○	○	○	○	○	○ very likely>
How likely are you to reuse the services of this library?	○	○	○	○	○	○	○	○	○	○

Please indicate the importance and your level of satisfaction with the following facilities available at the . . . library

	Satisfaction	Importance
Hours of access and operation	--Satisfaction-- ▸	--Importance-- ▸
Accessibility (transportation to/from and access within and into building)	--Satisfaction-- ▸	--Importance-- ▸
Seating/Workspace	--Satisfaction-- ▸	--Importance-- ▸
Personal safety and security	--Satisfaction-- ▸	--Importance-- ▸
Building interior	--Satisfaction-- ▸	--Importance-- ▸
Maintenance and cleanliness: Building exterior	--Satisfaction-- ▸	--Importance-- ▸
Exterior grounds and spaces	--Satisfaction-- ▸	--Importance-- ▸
Restrooms	--Satisfaction-- ▸	--Importance-- ▸
Dedicated spaces for: Children	--Satisfaction-- ▸	--Importance-- ▸

(Cont.)

Table 6.1 **Customer Satisfaction Survey: Selected Questions** (Cont.)

	Satisfaction	Importance
Teens	--Satisfaction-- ▶	--Importance-- ▶
Adults	--Satisfaction-- ▶	--Importance-- ▶
Meeting space/Program room	--Satisfaction-- ▶	--Importance-- ▶
Exterior courtyard or garden	--Satisfaction-- ▶	--Importance-- ▶
Please indicate your level of satisfaction with and the importance of the following equipment at this library . . .	Satisfaction	Importance
Printers	--Satisfaction-- ▶	--Importance-- ▶
Copiers	--Satisfaction-- ▶	--Importance-- ▶
Catalogue terminals	--Satisfaction-- ▶	--Importance-- ▶
Catalogue/Database stations	--Satisfaction-- ▶	--Importance-- ▶
Self-checkout stations	--Satisfaction-- ▶	--Importance-- ▶

These questions are reprinted from Peter Hernon and Ellen Altman, *Assessing Service Quality: Satisfying the Expectations of Library Customers* (Chicago: American Library Association, 2010), 143–47. Those pages include the entire questionnaire. Reprinted with permission of Counting Opinions.

As parts of two categories, plan and response rate, libraries want to develop an ongoing dialogue with customers and demonstrate a willingness to listen and act on what they learn. Hearing is not the same as listening; in other words, receiving sounds is not the same as paying attention to and acting on them. Act does not mean doing whatever customers say. When libraries do not initiate change based on some of the study findings, they need to communicate this to their communities and maintain an ongoing dialogue. As libraries plan the survey, they should challenge themselves to gain a high response rate and not settle for one much less than 50 percent. To do so, they need to answer questions such as the following before they engage in actual data collection:

- How do we frame the imposition to get people to respond and to do so thoughtfully?
- Why will busy people take the time to complete the survey, especially a long one?

Customer Comments

Surveys and other data collection instruments might include a question soliciting actual customer comments. In some instances, libraries might want to package favorable comments as testimonials and to create stories based on those testimonials. For instance, the library might cull the comments for mention of increased weekend hours of being open to the public. The goal might be increased hours if the mayor and city council will provide extra funding. Testimonials allow the library to relate what community residents say in their own words. Still, the library should be sensitive to any concern that its mangers cherry-picked favorable comments. The critical question is, "What do library managers do with less favorable comments?"

Box 6.3 draws on comments that public library customers actually made as part of a customer satisfaction survey. Some of the comments in the data set are complaints about rude or impolite behavior on the part of some staff, calls for both quiet and noisy areas, expressions of likes and dislikes, disruption caused by the homeless, and suggestions for book purchases. How often do customers mention each; when problems are expressed, what are the patterns and how often is there recurrence?

Some of the recurring comments might suggest topics for staff training. For the comments reported in the figure, what should managers do with them, and how do they report back to customers about action taken or not taken? It is interesting to note that a number of customers conclude their remarks with "thank you."

Box 6.3
Customer Comments

1. I am having difficulty logging in to your eBooks. Wish you had more audioBooks available

2. The programs offered in the Children's library are wonderful, and the book selection there is very good. It is a great resource for grandmothers like me, as well as parents and caregivers

3. My family is VERY interested in utilizing eBooks and similar resources. We are very tech savvy. However, to date, we have found deciphering the e-books system, selection, check-out procedures, etc. IMPOSSIBLE to crack. The digital website needs to be clearer (step-by-step instructions, for specific common outcomes, please. E.G. "How do I check-out and load a book on my Kindle? My iPad?" I guess you should offer more frequent classes for e-books, and publicize. The online book request/renew/save lists, etc. is brilliant, and I recommend it often

4. I love the library. Thank you! The one thing I have to note is the overwhelming smell of mold at the Main Library and at the . . . [branch] library. I guess it's the smell of the books, not the building. But this overwhelming mold/mildew smell really gets me and I cannot stay in the library for very long. Thanks

5. I love the library! Thanks for being a great resource for the community

6. The . . . Library is the jewel in the crown of . . . [the city]. The library system works so well to serve so many. I am constantly astonished at the services provided and the efficiency of the library staff at all locations. I love the library system here in the city, and it is my most cherished benefit as a taxpayer and resident of . . . [the city]. Thank you

7. We were thrilled with the renovation of the . . . [branch] Library. The whole family enjoys visiting the library. When it reopened after the renovation the library had beautiful landscaping. My only question is who is responsible for the grounds? Tall weeds and trash now cover the landscaping

8. I have been coming here since I was ten years of age, So for 40 years it's been a great place to find resources! Thank you

9. Any time I can ever vote to keep our libraries alive and prosperous, I will do so

10. May I respectfully suggest that, where time and resources permit, perhaps more material could be available as eBooks or placed online to further minimize if not completely avoid instances of books being returned late. Where possible, additional computer terminals and access points could be utilized as secure terminals for people needing secure access to the Internet

11. I can't emphasize enough how important the . . . library is to me and our community. And the . . . branch rocks! . . . I'm proud that . . . [the city] supports our public library so consistently

12. Need more Internet terminals, cleaner workspaces, and cleaner restrooms

13. It saddens me that so many books are written in and in poor condition. As for the DVDs, how scratched can they get? When I pick them up I cannot see how scratched they are; most won't play for me. I wonder how much the library spends on them

14. The homeless situation both inside and outside the Main Library damages its reputation severely. I know a lot of people who won't use it because of that. It's a shame, because I think the collection is wonderful and should be used more widely. I visit the library as much as ever but don't stay there to read periodicals as I used to, because of the smells and noise, and that's a shame. I do applaud the security personnel for responding quickly to reports of disturbances, and all the staff for bearing up in a difficult situation. I'm proud and grateful that . . . [the city] continues to fund its libraries, as they are a valuable resource for me and the envy of friends in other cities

15. The library is satisfactory except for the homeless issue. They use the restrooms like a shower. They sleep, eat, and bother people who are trying to concentrate, study or just read. I'm a visitor here, and basically it leaves a bad reputation on the city. As for the library I can honestly say I will not return to . . . [the library] in the future!

16. I'm currently homeless. So, I appreciate what the library has to offer. The 15 minute computers are great to keep checking e-mail and send resumes throughout the day. Overall, this library is very competent and caring of all who seek help here. Thank you very much

Customer Satisfaction Index

The American Customer Satisfaction Index, www.theacsi.org/, is perhaps the best-known series of satisfaction indexes as it covers 47 industries, more than 200 companies, and more than 100 federal and local government agencies and services. Offering a broad presentation of the U.S. economy, it reports scores on a scale ranging up to 100 and suggests the causes and consequences of customer satisfaction. Some libraries have created their own index that, among other things, covers customer satisfaction for the main and branch libraries. However, any metrics produced might not be gathered on a regular basis and be announced on the library home page.

Customer Satisfaction Metrics

Customer satisfaction is a complex issue, one that cannot be completely divorced from employee satisfaction, and it might involve any aspect of a library's infrastructure (collections and other services, facilities, staff, and technology). The metrics discussed in this section provide an overview and should not be viewed as the sole reflection of satisfaction. Still, given the national attention accorded to them, they are far from unimportant. These metrics might be used to benchmark performance so that library managers can introduce corrections and determine the extent to which performance improved.

NET PROMOTER SCORE

The Net Promoter Score (NPS), a loyalty metric developed by Fred Reichheld of Bain & Company, tracks how customers characterize a company to others. For a question such as "How likely are you to recommend (our company) to a colleague or friend?," which respondents choose from a ten-point scale to answer, he classified scores into three categories:

1. 1–6 as detractors;
2. 7–8 as passives (neutral); and
3. 9–10 as promoters.

In the case of libraries, promoters are very supportive customers who encourage others to use the library and its myriad of services. Detractors are the opposite; they want little to do with the library, have low expectations, and are probably infrequent users. Reichheld calculated the NPS by subtracting the percentage of detractors from the percentage of promoters, while ignoring the passives:

NPS = % of Promoters − % of Detractors

This metric has its critics,[3] but it offers a unique way to interpret survey responses. However, when determining the NPS, librarians should not forget to place the resulting percentage(s) in the context of two questions:

1. Would you recommend the services of this library to others?
2. How likely are you to reuse the services of this library?

If library managers can pinpoint individuals characterized as promoters and detractors, they might conduct focus group interviews with some members of each group. They might also convert the focus groups into panels and meet with members on a recurring basis. Still, it is important to determine what comprises a good and, conversely, a bad score. There is no magic percentage that an organization needs to achieve; a percentage of 50, or lower, is not necessarily bad.[4] In a study of the NPS for public libraries, Joseph R. Matthews found that "promoters are very frequent library users, are adults, and ascribe a high value to the library. Detractors are typically first-time library users, are not likely to return, have multiple library cards (and thus compare collections and services that they receive), and are likely to be students."[5] This example illustrates how it is important to know who comprises promoters and detractors.

OPPORTUNITY INDEX

Anthony W. Ulwick developed an Opportunity Index,[6] which applies gap analysis (customer importance and satisfaction) to produce a rank-order list (high to low) of service areas that customers perceive as needing improvement. As shown in box 6.4, the index

= Importance (mean score) + Importance (mean score)

– Satisfaction (mean score)

Or,

= Importance (mean score) – Satisfaction (mean score)

+ Importance (mean score)

Box 6.4

Calculating the Opportunity Index

This index, which complements the Net Promoter Score, compares questions that address both importance and satisfaction so that managers can examine the gap in the context of the fifth gap, Gaps Model of Service Quality (see figure 6.1). Importance is the theoretical matter of greatest importance to "customers."

The first two questions in table 6.1 cover the following:

1. Overall how important is this library to you?
2. Overall, how satisfied are you with the services of this library?

Step One

Find the mean score for each question. The mean is the sum of all the scores divided by the number of scores

Step Two

Take the mean for question 1 (importance) and add it *twice*. So, if the mean for that question is 6.133, add 6.133 for a total of 12.266

Step Three

If the mean score for question 2 is 4.222, subtract that value from 12.266. The answer is 8.044

Step Four

We now have a value that we can compare to other sets of questions that deal with *both* importance and satisfaction

Step Five

For each question in table 6.1 relating to facilities, find the mean for both satisfaction and importance (repeat steps one-three)

Step Six

Array the values for step three for questions 1, 2, and those relating to facilities, from highest to lowest. Those questions with the very highest mean scores—those above the "overall importance and satisfaction" (step three for questions 1 and 2)—become the areas to focus on in the Opportunity Index. Following is part of a hypothetical:

SERVICE	OPPORTUNITY INDEX (MEAN)
Books and other materials to borrow/reference	11.85
Access to e-books	10.9
Hours of access and operation	10.64
Catalog/database stations	9.97
Seating/workspace	9.96
Overall importance and satisfaction*	9.77

*Step three for questions 1 and 2.

The Opportunity Index can be applied across organizations or within an organization. Regardless, as Ulwick points out, "selecting the richest areas of opportunities from a long list . . . is critical, since chasing after less promising ones drains resources."[7]

Libraries may want to create another series of questions to add to table 6.1 that can be calculated and inserted into the Opportunity Index. They might ask customers about levels of importance and satisfaction about types of resources, such as print books, audiobooks, DVDs, music CDs, and e-books.

OTHER METRICS

Three other metrics might be reported on a recurring basis. First, the above-mentioned question about willingness to recommend the services of this library might become *recommend rate*. To calculate the rate, managers might compare individuals answering 9 or 10 (on a ten-point scale) to the rest of the respondents. Second, the above-mentioned reuse question might be similarly characterized (*reuse rate*). Both the recommend and reuse rates might also be expressed in terms of the NPS, promoters and detractors. Third, *resolution rate* refers to those individuals completing a comment card, making a comment in a suggestion box—online or otherwise—or making critical comments in a survey, e-mail message, or social network. This rate refers, first, to the percentage of those making comments in relation to the percentage of individuals identifying themselves; and second, the percentage of self-identifiers for whom there is successful resolution of the problem.

Before library managers calculate the recommend and reuse rates, they need to decide what comprises a good or bad rate. Further, how does that rate compare to other metrics they deem important?

Concluding Thoughts

When someone thinks of customer service and delighting customers, the private sector comes to mind, in particular companies such as the Ritz-Carleton Hotel chain or L. L. Bean. The Ritz-Carleton is committed to "wowing" or delighting customers and ensuring a memorable service experience—the hotel is more than a place to stay. We are not suggesting that libraries adopt the WOW philosophy, but they should include a customer service component in their strategic and other plans and commit the entire organization to achieving high-quality service. As the Public Library Association notes,

> If you Google "customer service in public libraries" you'll get more than 19 million results. WorldCat comes up with 473 hits for the same phrase. . . . It's one thing to say that your library will offer good customer service; it's another to ensure that everyone associated with the library (staff, board, Friends) practices it.[8]

For libraries and many service industries high customer satisfaction is an important part of customer service, in part because it helps an organization retain customers and expand its customer base in a highly competitive marketplace. Increasingly stakeholders are asking about satisfaction and expecting service organizations to report on it in times of restricted fiscal commitments. More libraries are expected to do more with fewer resources, without sacrificing customer satisfaction. It merits mention that administrators (e.g., college or university presidents and provosts, mayors, and city councilors) might have a simplistic definition of satisfaction—they do not receive complaints about library collections and services. However, regardless of the circumstances, survey results, be they for customer satisfaction or service quality (the next chapter), must be linked to ongoing service improvements and resource reallocation.

Exercises

NET PROMOTER SCORE

NPS = % of Promoters (scores of 9, 10)
− % of Detractors (scores of 1–6)

Overall, how important is this library to you?

Data (January–December 2011):

    1 (9 responses), 2 (4 responses), 3 (9 responses),
    4 (13 responses), 5 (53 responses), 6 (112 responses),
    7 (186 responses), 8 (418 responses), 9 (549 responses),
    10 (2130 responses). Total: 3,483

Data (January–December 2012):

    1 (15 responses), 2 (7 responses), 3 (12 responses),
    4 (18 responses), 5 (62 responses), 6 (119 responses),
    7 (176 responses), 8 (512 responses), 9 (514 responses),
    10 (2012 responses): Total: 3,447

Data (January–June 2013):

    1 (7 responses), 2 (4 responses), 3 (6 responses),
    4 (11 responses), 5 (44 responses), 6 (61 responses),
    7 (86 responses), 8 (312 responses), 9 (314 responses),
    10 (1002 responses): Total: 1,847

Overall, how satisfied are you with the services of this library?

Data (January–December 2011):

> 1 (23 responses), 2 (27 responses), 3 (42 responses),
> 4 (42 responses), 5 (126 responses), 6 (218 responses),
> 7 (308 responses), 8 (680 responses), 9 (715 responses),
> 10 (1,038 responses). Total: 3,219

Data (January–December 2012):

> 1 (18 responses), 2 (20 responses), 3 (44 responses),
> 4 (38 responses), 5 (121 responses), 6 (219 responses),
> 7 (298 responses), 8 (567 responses), 9 (679 responses),
> 10 (1,292 responses): Total: 3,296

Data (January–June 2013):

> 1 (5 responses), 2 (7 responses), 3 (4 responses),
> 4 (8 responses), 5 (23 responses), 6 (48 responses),
> 7 (46 responses), 8 (201 responses), 9 (189 responses),
> 10 (678 responses): Total: 1,209

1. Calculate the NPS for:
   - 2011
   - 2012
   - January–June 2013

2. What conclusions can you draw from what the NPS calculated?

3. What do you do with the results? Anything actionable? Would you display the results on the home page, and so on? Why yes/no? If yes, how would you display the results?

The initial set of questions also includes: "How well do these services compare to your expectations?" and "Overall how do you rate the quality of these services?" Do you see these as amenable to analysis with the NPS? Discuss. How would you display the results?

How well do these services compare to your expectations?

Data (January–December 2012):

1 (28 responses), 2 (42 responses), 3 (57 responses),
4 (77 responses), 5 (164 responses), 6 (296 responses),
7 (336 responses), 8 (587responses), 9 (662 responses),
10 (957 responses): Total: 3,182

Overall how do you rate the quality of these services?

Data (January–December 2012):

1 (23 responses), 2 (33 responses), 3 (40 responses),
4 (59 responses), 5 (118 responses), 6 (230 responses),
7 (324 responses), 8 (663 responses), 9 (678 responses),
10 (1,029 responses): Total: 3,197

For both questions, calculate the NPS and interpret the results?

OPPORTUNITY INDEX

OI = Importance (mean score) + Importance (mean score)
− Satisfaction (mean score)

For the time period, July–December 2012, responses to the questions in table 6.1 were as follows:

Overall, how important is this library to you?

1 (4 responses), 2 (1 response), 3 (1 response),
4 (1 response), 5 (2 responses), 6 (4 responses),
7 (6 responses), 8 (14 responses), 9 (21 responses),
10 (211 responses). Total: 265

Overall, how satisfied are you with the services of this library?

1 (8 responses), 2 (0 responses), 3 (3 responses),
4 (6 responses), 5 (6 responses), 6 (11 responses),
7 (27 responses), 8 (41 responses), 9 (37 responses),
10 (118 responses). Total: 257

Hours of access and operation (importance):

> 1 (44 responses), 2 (4 responses), 3 (8 responses),
> 4 (7 responses), 5 (14 responses), 6 (16 responses),
> 7 (15 responses), 8 (22 responses), 9 (13 responses),
> 10 (54 responses). Total: 197

Hours of access and operation (satisfaction):

> 1 (8 responses), 2 (2 responses), 3 (6 responses),
> 4 (7 responses), 5 (21 responses), 6 (14 responses),
> 7 (17 responses), 8 (14 responses), 9 (17 responses),
> 10 (65 responses). Total: 171

Naturally, for the remaining questions that ascertain both importance and satisfaction, the same process of determining the mean score would be followed. This example, however, stops at this point, as the principle has been illustrated.

4. Calculate the scores and insert into an Opportunity Index.

RECOMMEND RATE

Recommend rate = % (9 or 10) to % for the rest of the respondents.
An alternative is to calculate and report the mean

5. Let's assume that for the time period, January–December 2011, a total of 3,183 customers completed this question and the breakdown was: 1 (28 responses), 2 (27 responses), 3 (29 responses), 4 (39 responses), 5 (85 responses), 6 (180 responses), 7 (167 responses), 8 (349 responses), 9 (512 responses), and 10 (1,767 responses). What is the recommend rate?

6. Let's further assume that for the time period, January–December 2012, a total of 3,648 customers completed this question and the breakdown was: 1 (33 responses), 2 (39 responses), 3 (18 responses), 4 (14 responses), 5 (82 responses), 6 (130 responses), 7 (181 responses), 8 (153 responses), 9 (347 responses), and 10 (2,651 responses). What is the recommend rate?

7. Further, for the time period, January–June, 2013, a total of 1,221 customers completed this question and the breakdown was: 1 (19 responses), 2 (17 responses), 3 (24 responses), 4 (12 responses), 5 (29 responses), 6 (168 responses), 7 (22 responses), 8 (99 responses), 9 (33 responses), and 10 (798 responses). What is the reuse rate?

8. Review questions 5–7; what pattern emerges? How would you explain those patterns? Remember to determine the extent to which you consider the rate good or bad. Why do you characterize it as good or otherwise?

9. How would you display the results and where would you place them (e.g., on the home page)?

REUSE RATE

Reuse rate = % (marking 9 or 10) to % for the rest of the respondents. An alternative is to calculate and report the mean.

10. Let's assume that for the time period, January–December 2011, a total of 3,147 customers completed this question and the breakdown was: 1 (21 responses), 2 (24 responses), 3 (23 responses), 4 (22 responses), 5 (66 responses), 6 (135 responses), 7 (91 responses), 8 (187 responses), 9 (333 responses), and 10 (2,245 responses). What is the reuse rate?

11. Let's further assume that for the time period, January December 2012, a total of 3,394 customers completed this question and the breakdown was: 1 (17 responses), 2 (19 responses), 3 (20 responses), 4 (16 responses), 5 (75 responses), 6 (140 responses), 7 (81 responses), 8 (173 responses), 9 (353 responses), and 10 (2,500 responses). What is the reuse rate?

12. Further, for the time period, January–June, 2013, a total of 1,595 customers completed this question and the breakdown was: 1 (16 responses), 2 (13 responses), 3 (21 responses), 4 (14 responses), 5 (26 responses), 6 (134 responses), 7 (37 responses), 8 (99 responses), 9 (137 responses), and 10 (1,098 responses). What is the reuse rate?

13. Review questions 9–11. What pattern emerges? How would you explain those patterns? Remember to determine the extent to which you consider the rate good or bad. Why do you characterize it as good or otherwise?

14. How would you display the results and where would you place them (e.g., on the home page)?

RESOLUTION RATE

Resolution rate (individuals completing a comment card, making a comment otherwise) = % of those making comments in relation to % of individuals identifying themselves

NOTE: It is possible that library managers may want to track this rate by source of comment (e.g., comment card or social networks)

15. Let's assume that the library has comment cards scattered throughout the library and an online suggestion form and that for 2012, there were 123 comments, 60 of which appeared in comment cards and the remaining 73 in the online form. Of the 60 comments, 10 included contact information and for the 73, 29 did so. Of the 10, 5 offered critical comments, and of the 29, 10 did so. The library was able to resolve the issues to the customer's satisfaction in 3 (of 5) and 10 (of 15) instances. What is the resolution rate?

    Let's also assume that the customers in box 6.3 made those comments. Do you see any patterns to the comments that require action, whether a resolution or communication to the community of customers? Explain.

(Answers to these questions are in the "Appendix" at the back of the book. We encourage different members of a library staff to work on the exercises together and to discuss the results.)

NOTES

1. Peter Hernon and Joseph R. Matthews, *Listening to the Customer* (Santa Barbara, CA: Libraries Unlimited, 2011).

2. Peter Hernon and Ellen Altman, *Assessing Service Quality: Satisfying the Expectations of Library Customers* (Chicago: American Library Association, 2010), 149–50.

3. See *Vovici* blog, "The Listening Post: "Net Promoter Score (NPS) Criticisms and Best Practices" (April 28, 2009), http://blog.vovici.com/blog/bid/18204/Net-Promoter-Score-NPS-Criticisms-and-Best-Practices.

4. See Joseph R. Matthews, "Customer Satisfaction: A New Perspective," *Public Libraries* 47, no. 6 (November/December 2008): 52–55.

5. Ibid., 53.

6. Anthony Ulwick, "Turn Customer Input into Innovation," *Harvard Business Review* 80, no. 1 (January 2002): 91–97.

7. Ibid., 96.

8. Public Library Association, "The Not-So-Secret Keys to Great Customer Service," *Public Libraries Online*, www.publiclibrariesonline.org/content/not-so-secret-keys-great-customer-service.

MEASURING SERVICE QUALITY

The importance of service quality, which is an antecedent of customer satisfaction, cannot be overemphasized. Higher service quality leads to increased levels of customer satisfaction. Richard Orr, an early proponent of identifying the quality of libraries, distinguishes between quality and value. The former, he indicates, should reflect how good the service is in comparison to value, which focuses on how much good the service does.[1] Service quality has two components, both of which are important: what is provided to customers and how the service is delivered, or deliverables and interactions. Deliverables describe what is provided to customers, and interactions describe the characteristics of staff and equipment that impact how customers experience the service process.

Similar to customer satisfaction, the concept of service quality is based on the Gaps Model of Services (see figure 6.1). The components of the model include aspects provided by the service provider—the library— and the customer. The model recognizes that expectations are subjective, change over time, and are not predictable. Customers compare their expectations with their perceptions of actual performance and find that they are

- confirmed when perceived performance meets expectations;
- affirmed when perceived performance exceeds expectations; or
- disconfirmed (failed by negative disconfirmation) when perceived performance falls short of expectations.

Expectations of excellent service arise in the customers' minds based on their experiences with other service organizations as well as the expectations they form based on their prior contacts with the library. Consequently, from the customer's perspective, a service quality gap arises from the difference between the perceived service and the expected service. An understanding gap arises from the differences between the customer's service expectations and management's understanding of what customers expect. That gap might be a design, delivery, or communications gap. A design gap appears due to management's misunderstanding of customer expectations and the service design, resources, and specifications that management plans to provide. A delivery gap occurs when there is a gap between the specification of service quality and the actual quality of service delivered, and a communications gap materializes as the result of what is actually delivered and what has been promised (implied or stated) in terms of library communications to the customer.

Jeffrey E. Disend, who correlates the Gaps Model with the concept of service quality, maintains that poor service results if the gap, or difference, is large between what is expected and what is delivered. When what is delivered matches what is expected, customers find the service acceptable. If the service is better than what they expected, exceptional service materializes.[2] Consequently, when expectations and perceptions are ranked on a scale, the gap is a number reflecting the difference between the two—exceptions ranking minus perceptions ranking. If there is a poor service gap, a negative number occurs. If the number, by chance, is zero, service is acceptable (expectations and perceptions match). If a positive value emerges (perceptions exceed expectations) and the greater that value is, the service provided has achieved exceptional service.

Using Surveys

Service quality was first studied through marketing research in the profit sector. The SERVQUAL instrument defines *service quality* as perceived quality rather than *objective quality* and compares the expectations of customers and the service performance using the following dimensions:

> **Tangibles,** which include such aspects as the physical appearance of the library, library staff members, equipment, and communication materials (signage, handouts, and so forth);
>
> **Reliability,** which refers to service reliability and the consistency of service;
>
> **Responsiveness,** which evaluates how timely the service is provided and how willing the staff is to meet the needs of their customers;
>
> **Assurance,** which addresses the competence and confidence of staff, their knowledge, professionalism, and courteousness;
>
> **Empathy,** which examines staff willingness to address individual customer needs in a warm and supportive manner.

Within libraries, SERVQUAL was replaced with LibQUAL+ and the dimensions pared down to:

> **Affect of service, the human aspect,** which relates to the extent to which library staff are courteous, knowledgeable, helpful, and reliable;
>
> **Information control,** which measures how customers prefer to interact with the library and whether the needed information is delivered in the format, location, and time of their choosing; and
>
> **Library as a place,** which covers the usefulness of space, the symbolic value of the library, and the library as a refuge for work or study.

In reviewing the literature on service quality, both within and outside library and information science, three distinct approaches to data collection emerge, all of which rely on surveying customers. In the first, customers receive and rate a predetermined list of service statements and the five attributes associated with SERVQUAL. However, some of the statements might be tailored to the local situation. Nonetheless, the intention is to compare service industries from the customer perspective. In the second approach, libraries contract with the Association of Research Libraries to administer LibQUAL+. The final approach applies the concept of customer service and the interactive relationship between a library and the people whom it is supposed to serve. How the library sees and interacts with its customers affects the quality and nature of the services rendered. As a result, individual libraries select only those statements of potentially greatest value to their customers, determine which ones to integrate into their services, and link the evaluation to the planning process. In essence, libraries create their own SERVQUAL or LibQUAL+.

Regardless of the approach taken, as expectations change service organizations need to engage more in resource review and allocation on a regular basis. As Françoise Hébert points out, "When library and customer measures of quality are not congruent, the library may be meeting its internal standards of performance but may not be performing well in the eyes of its customers."[3] Based on her quote, we ask, "What are the implications of having such an organization?"

LIBQUAL+

Developed in 1999 by libraries affiliated with the Association of Research Libraries (ARL), the survey instrument includes twenty-two questions providing information about the three dimensions. Respondents answer each question using a Likert scale of one to nine, complete some demographic questions, and can add comments to a series of open-ended questions.[4] In addition, there is an opportunity to add some locally oriented questions. The aim of the survey, a web-based survey (however, some participants prefer to complete a paper version), is to

- Assist librarians in understanding user perceptions of library service quality better;
- Gather and analyze user feedback systematically over time;
- Provide a library with comparable data from peer institutions;
- Foster a culture of excellence in providing library services;
- Identify and introduce best practices in library services; and
- Enhance staff analytical skills for interpreting and acting on data.

After all, gathering a significant amount of data and then not acting on them is not only wasteful of resources but raises user expectations (only to have them dashed on the shoals of reality when nothing changes in the library).[5]

More than a decade later, more than 1,000 libraries in the United States and other countries, predominately academic libraries, have completed the survey at least once. Many academic libraries schedule the use of LibQUAL on a two- to three-year cycle.

Survey respondents provide three answers to each question: "my minimum service level," "my desired service level," and "my perceived service level" (see note 4). The responses are then used to determine the size of different gaps: the difference between the minimum service level and the perceived service level, and the difference between the desired service level and the perceived service level. A library pays for the web-based survey each time it is used. ARL provides training assistance in setting up the survey as well as offering advice on encouraging higher response rates. Data are analyzed for all respondents. In addition, it is also possible to break down the data into various subgroups: undergraduates, graduate students, faculty, and so forth. ARL provides a standard report as a part of their service that compares one library's responses with the responses of all other participating libraries.[6]

LibQUAL+ Lite, a shorter version of the instrument, has all respondents answer selected survey core questions while only a randomly selected subsample respond to the remaining questions. In summary, data are collected on all questions, but each respondent completes only eight of the twenty-two core survey questions.[7]

Aside from tracking the service quality ratings over time, one of the real benefits of the survey, in either form, is that on average about 40 percent of the respondents provide some comments. However, someone needs to read and categorize the comments; fortunately, there are some full-text analysis tools (both proprietary and open source) that can assist in the full-text analysis. Many libraries have found real value in carefully analyzing and considering the feedback in the form of these open-ended questions from the library's customers.

One concern is about the degree to which the respondents are representative of the campus population as well as the overall sample size;

many libraries have less than a 20 percent response rate. Thus, it is difficult to generalize findings across a multicultural student body, one that
might have individuals with disabilities.[8] Further, with increased focus
on the Internet and web delivery of services and resources, the question
arises, "To what extent is a non-eLibQUAL still appropriate?" or "How
e-focused should LibQUAL be?" (See the section on "E-Service Quality"
below.)

OTHER SURVEYS

Rather than relying on LibQUAL+, a library could revert back to
SERVQUAL and create its own survey or one that has been used in
another library but on a highly selective basis. The primary benefit of
this approach is that the questions may be of more interest to a library's
management team than those found in the LibQUAL survey. However,
extreme caution should be exercised when going down this road. The
reason is that the survey instrument may not have been pretested to
ensure that respondents clearly understand the statements. Still, there
are examples:

> Danuta A. Nitecki and Peter Hernon combined the local approach
> to identify service factors with a version of SERVQUAL. Their
> study took place at Yale University libraries, and the success of
> their survey suggests that it can be replicated elsewhere. Central
> to their approach is that the statements or questions require modi-
> fication from setting to setting, as determined by the priorities for
> service improvement established by individual libraries and their
> management teams. The goal is local diagnosis built around state-
> ments that have importance to both a library and its customers.[9]

> Peter Hernon and Philip Calvert, in conjunction with specialists in
> the area of disabilities, modified the SERVQUAL instrument to be
> relevant to students with disabilities. They reported strategies to
> gather data from such students. Their findings indicate that instru-
> ments such as LibQUAL are not appropriate for such a population.[10]

> Some state libraries maintain a list of surveys, including customer
> satisfaction and service quality surveys that have been used in
> other library settings. See, for example, the Library Research Ser-
> vice of the Colorado State Library (www.lrs.org/usersurveys.php).

E-Service Quality

The exploration of e-service quality (e-SQ) in service industries has been under way since the first part of the last decade and has determined that the concept is multifaceted; its dimensions differ from those previously identified; and it affects satisfaction, the intent to purchase, and actual purchasing. Relevant dimensions might be related to website design, reliability, responsiveness, personalization, information, and empathy from the e-service provider's perspective, and trust and experience from the customer's perspective. At the same time, efficiency and fulfillment have become critical facets of website service quality for the private sector.[11]

In cooperation with librarians from different academic libraries, Hernon and Calvert developed an extensive set of statements from which libraries could select the few to probe or gain ideas about new statements to create. The goal was to develop an instrument relevant to local environments.[12]

Finally, ARL has started the development of DigiQUAL, www.digiqual .org/, which modifies LibQUAL+, to examine e-SQ, focusing on the dimension for information control. Examples of statements include "[web] site being intuitive," "easily finding information on the site," and "site facilitating self-directed research."[13] As of early 2013, Digi-QUAL had yet to be fully developed and thus is not yet available for libraries to use.

Other Means of Listening to Customers

In addition to surveys such as LibQUAL+, a library should obviously use a number of other ways to listen to the customer. Among the many methods that are available and have been used in a number of libraries, some deserve mention. These include the use of a suggestion box and/ or comment cards (both physical cards as well as an online form found on the library's website), telephone surveys, focus group interviews, and complaint tracking systems.[14] The use of multiple methods, often called triangulation, allows the library to create a richer and deeper understanding of the library's customers and the areas the library needs to improve—from the customer's perspective and often in the actual words of the customer.

Concluding Thoughts

Central to this and the preceding chapter is a survey in which librarians impose on customers and want their feedback. Before they employ this method for the first time or if previous surveys have not generated a high response rate, they might review key literature on survey methods and ensure that the instrument developed meets the type of checklist presented in Assessing Service Quality.[15] Any surveys such as those associated with customer satisfaction or service quality should be performed on a regular basis so that customers become accustomed to and appreciate libraries listening to what they say. Active listening does not necessarily mean accepting or acting on something; rather, there is an ongoing dialogue between libraries and their customers.

Exercises

1. Review the various e-SQ statements in the Hernon and Calvert article (note 12) and develop/select twenty that would be worthy of probing with your library customers. Why these twenty? How might data collected be used to improve e-SQ?

2. Differentiate between service quality and satisfaction.

3. How is service quality related to the concept of customer service?

4. Identify the relative strengths and limitations of the SERVQUAL and LibQUAL instruments. Which one would work best in your library setting, and why?

5. A LibQUAL or SERVQUAL instrument might contain statements that library managers could turn into customer-related metrics. Returning to exercise 1 or to an instrument that does not concentrate on the e-environment, develop two such metrics. Example: "Library staff are welcoming when customers approach them and request assistance." The metric is:

   Number of staff who are welcoming/Number of staff approached

Next, discuss how you would collect data to insert into that metric. How reliable and valid might the data be?

6. Building from the previous question, are there some metrics that might be gathered without imposing on customers to participate in a survey or interview? In other words, might the staff develop some metrics from observation? Discuss.

(Answers to these questions are in the "Appendix" at the back of the book. We encourage different members of a library staff to work on the exercises together and to discuss the results.)

NOTES

1. Richard Orr, "Measuring the Goodness of Library Services," *Journal of Documentation* 29, no. 3 (1973): 315–52.

2. Jeffrey E. Disend, *How to Provide Excellent Service in Any Organization: A Blueprint for Making All the Theories Work* (Radnor, PA: Chilton Book, 1991), 108.

3. Françoise Hébert, "Service Quality: An Unobtrusive Investigation of Interlibrary Loan in Large Public Libraries in Canada," *Library & Information Science Research* 16, no. 1 (1994): 20.

4. Examples of statements included on the instrument are "Employees who instill confidence in users"; "Library space that inspires study and learning"; "Employees who are consistently courteous"; and "A library website enabling me to locate information on my own." Respondents rate these statements from 1 (the lowest) to 9 (the highest) by indicating: *Minimum Service Level*: the number that represents the minimum level of service that you would find acceptable; *Desired Service Level*: the number that represents the level of service that you personally want; and *Perceived Service Performance*: the number that represents the level of service that you believe our library currently provides.

5. Association of Research Libraries, "General Information: What Is LibQUAL+®" (2013), www.libqual.org/about/about_lq/general_info.

6. Peter Hernon and Ellen Altman, *Assessing Service Quality: Satisfying the Expectations of Library Customers* (Chicago: American Library Association, 2010), 161.

7. See Association of Research Libraries, "LibQUAL+® Lite" (2013), www.libqual.org/about/about_lq/LQ_lite.

8. See Peter Hernon and Philip Calvert, *Improving the Quality of Library Services for Students with Disabilities* (Westport, CT: Libraries Unlimited, 2006).

9. Danuta A. Nitecki and Peter Hernon, "Measuring Service Quality at Yale University Libraries," *Journal of Academic Librarianship* 26, no. 4 (2000): 257–73.

10. Hernon and Calvert, *Improving the Quality of Library Services for Students with Disabilities*.

11. A. Parasuraman, Valarie A. Zeithaml, and Arvind Malhotra, "E-S-QUAL: A Multiple-Item Scale for Assessing Electronic Service Quality," *Journal of Service Research* 7 (2005): 1–21, http://public.kenan-flagler.unc.edu/faculty/malhotra/E-S-QualJServRsch.pdf.

12. Peter Hernon and Philip Calvert, "E-Service Quality in Libraries: Exploring Its Features and Dimensions," *Library & Information Science Research* 72, no. 3 (2005): 377–404.

13. Martha Kyrillidou, Bruce Thompson, and Colleen Cook, "Regrouping LibQUAL+® for the Digital Library Environment," paper presented at the 9th Northumbria International Conference on Performance Measurement in Libraries and Information Services, York, England, 2011, www.libqual.org/documents/LibQual/publications/digiqual.pdf.

14. Peter Hernon and Joseph R. Matthews, *Listening to the Customer* (Santa Barbara, CA: Libraries Unlimited, 2011).

15. Hernon and Altman, *Assessing Service Quality*, 108.

8

MEASURING RETURN ON INVESTMENT (ROI)

igher education institutions and almost every local community have been making substantial investments in their libraries for many generations. Library buildings have been designed and built, collections have been created and maintained, staff hired to provide a broad array of services, and more recently libraries have provided access to assorted information technologies. These investments have resulted in improvements to library collections, both print and electronic; services; and facilities. Yet, every library faces competitive pressure resulting in a tug-of-war for funding with other departments and the continual need to justify its funding and even its existence. For many decades, libraries enjoyed the support of their communities and funding decision makers because they were viewed as a public good with obvious positive social impacts—a public good is a service that is difficult to exclude someone from using and that one person's use does not deny someone else the use of that good or service. One of the ironies of funding in the public sector is that the library often takes a disproportionate budget hit, as compared to other departments, just when the economic downturn prompted an increase in demand for library programs and services. Today, there is increasing pressure for a library to articulate its tangible and intangible value to interested stakeholders such as funding decision makers, university administrators, and the community at large.

The traditional justifications for library funding, typically output metrics (e.g., the amount of annual circulation) used to demonstrate value, are not as effective as they once were. Stakeholders and communities now look for other indicators of value, one of which is a return on investment (ROI) analysis. In simple terms, a ROI analysis, often times called a cost-benefit analysis, estimates and compares the costs and benefits of an undertaking. Such an analysis can be used in any or all of three ways:

1. As a planning tool in choosing among alternatives and allocating scarce resources among competing demands;
2. As an evaluation tool to study an existing project or service; or
3. As a way to develop quantitative support in order to influence a funding decision.

Costs are much easier to determine, assuming an effort has been made to identify and include all relevant recurring and nonrecurring costs. It is difficult to calculate or estimate the value of the benefits of a service accurately and to determine that those benefits will occur for future years. Positive thinking, or unsubstantiated assumptions, may lead to underestimating the time and costs to complete a project or achieve some goal related to the strategic plan. Given this reality, it is not surprising that many cost-benefit analysis reports show a bias: benefits invariably exceed costs.[1]

Value is the worth of a product or service in terms of organizational, operational, social, and financial benefits to the customer. All library product offerings and services, whether in the physical library or delivered electronically, have a real value and cost in the mind of the customer. In addition to the actual out-of-pocket costs of getting to the library, other cost factors include the time and effort to use a library service. In effect a customer performs a quick cost-benefit analysis when considering the potential use of the library. The person does this by asking: "Do the benefits exceed the costs?" or "Is it worth my time?"

Most studies have estimated the economic value of library use by means of the criterion "maximize the ratio of benefits over costs." A report that discusses the value of the library in terms of ROI usually makes a statement such as "for every dollar supporting the library, the library sees a return on investment of X dollars" (almost always more than one dollar).

A means for measuring the economic value of libraries is consumer surplus, which emphasizes what customers, when surveyed, place on a library good or service in excess of what they would be willing to pay to purchase the service from an alternative source if the library service is not available. The consumer surplus is equal to the difference between what users would have been willing to pay and the assigned market price. The rationale is that library users enjoy a relative bargain of services available from the library when compared to their market price.[2]

One type of consumer surplus assessment is contingent valuation, in which survey respondents express an opinion about a library service directly by providing a subjective valuation of how much they would pay for that service, or, alternatively, how much they would accept in the form of tax savings if that or other services were eliminated. Contingent valuation uses two forms of questioning: willingness to pay (WTP) and willingness to accept (WTA). The first asks how much individuals would be willing to pay for a library service were they required to pay for it; the other focuses on how much money they would accept in order to forgo the good or service.[3]

Another approach to determine customer-centric economic benefit is by measuring user investment such as in access. A library saves customers' time by helping them find information faster than they could otherwise; time might also be viewed as time not wasted attempting to re-create data already available. However, library services tend to overlook the time users spend in accessing and using services. Such services may be provided free at the point of access to users, but users still invest in terms of their time to use these services.[4] To capture time data, managers assign a cost value to the length of time it takes to travel to use a service as well as the time spent in the library utilizing resources and services. These cost of time valuations posit that customers would not spend an hour of time in the library if they did not get at least as much out of it as they could get out of an hour of work.[5]

Determining the consumer surplus valuation from the customer's perspective may involve significant costs to the library because it is likely the library will need to contract with a third-party consultant or firm to conduct the survey and to produce the analysis and results. As an alternative, libraries may choose to calculate the valuation on behalf of their customers. This consumer surplus approach also focuses on the economic benefit or the financial amount the user saves relative to the costs of obtaining services from alternate sources. However, rather than the customers providing a value estimate, the library calculates the value of services, often based on use, and often applying costs lower than the cost of equivalent commercially available services. Value is calculated using the business sector's production of a commodity:

Value = Quantity (of the commodity produced) times
Price per Unit (of the commodity) or V = Q × P

In the case of the library, value equals the quantity of the commodity produced times the price unit of the commodity. A variant of this formula recognizes the value of a library benefit (resource or service) as evidenced by its use:

value of usage = measured output of a service multiplied
by the assigned price per unit, or Vu = MO × AP

A calculated value of usage could, as an example, be the number of books circulated times the price per book. A counter measures the output, and the price per unit can be assigned by the library, customers, or with an accepted benchmark. If 10,000 books were circulated, and the assigned price is $25.00 per book, the value of usage to the user is $250,000. Other values of usage could be calculated for borrowing other formats such as DVDs and audio recordings, or for downloading electronic formats such as music, books, or articles.

A library-calculated aggregate value of usage could be the sum from the assigned value for two or more of the most-used services. The aggregate value of usage in dollars (e.g., $50,000,000) is stated for a year, and may be compared on an annual basis using a time series chart. Several libraries provide an opportunity for users to calculate their own valuation. The library calculates the value of the services presented on a user-accessible web-based calculator; the user enters a value for the number of times he or she uses a service included on the calculator, including zero for nonuse. The calculator sums the value of the services used, and presents the user with the sum of personal value received from the library.[6] Another type of value calculator allows a library to identify the specific costs of each service in the community and then calculate the total value of the library to the community based on actual use figures.

Another interesting perspective is to provide a student return on investment calculation as the University of West Florida Libraries have done (see figure 8.1). The objective is to demonstrate, from the student's perspective, the value for some of the activities and services a student typically might use during the course of an academic year. The methods used to determine value for each service are available for downloading for interested parties.

Most of the data are readily available and are usually reported to the state library or to a professional association each year. The library may also display the average contribution per person made to the library for library services. Customers can then calculate their personal ROI by subtracting their calculated personal valuation of library services from their contribution to the library. If the summed personal valuation is greater than the contribution, there is a positive return on their investment for library services.

A best practice is to be as conservative as possible when assigning a market value to a library service. For example, the library decides to assign a value for books borrowed from its general collection. The average cost for a book is found in tables from *The Library and Book Trade Almanac* (formerly entitled *The Bowker Annual of Library and Book Trade Information*). The library takes that cost and then reduces it to a lower-than-100 percent figure to reflect the cost of a used book. Therefore, the library may assign a value to a circulating book that is 20 percent of the average cost of a new book.

It is important to state that value of usage is a proxy for evaluating the library's quality. The reason for undertaking the evaluation is to demonstrate how the library supports the institution's mission and its impact on individuals and the community, as well as to communicate this information to stakeholders in a meaningful and understandable manner.

Figure 8.1   Student Return on Investment

Anyone wanting to calculate a personal ROI should see
http://libguides.uwf.edu/content.php?pid=188487&sid=2261667.

Economic Benefits

By examining the possible economic benefits of using a library from the customer's perspective, it is possible to consider three categories of benefits:

1. **Direct use benefits:** Output and outcomes that can be measured directly. Some writers call a direct benefit a tangible benefit.

2. **Indirect use benefits** or economic impact: the intangible outputs and outcomes of a library are facilitated by programs and services.

3. **Nonuse benefits:** economists have recognized that individuals, who make no use of a public good, such as a public library, might derive satisfaction from its mere existence.

The total value of the library to the residents of a community or university, in theory, is determined by summing the use and nonuse benefits. All library product offerings and services have a real value and cost in the mind of the customer.

DIRECT USE BENEFITS

People have a reason for wanting to use the physical or virtual library, and they derive value based on the results of their interaction. The top three aspects of value or results revolve around the time saved, the money saved (or increased revenues), and accomplishments (better decisions and so forth).[7] In any library, benefits can be (or should be) identified for individual customers and all customers. The direct benefits for an individual who uses the public library focus on the avoidance of cost to the individual. These benefits include:

- Cost savings from not having to purchase materials (e.g., books, CDs, DVDs, magazine, newspapers, reference materials, and electronic resources);
- Free or low-cost access to computers, photocopiers, audio and video equipment, meeting rooms, programs, instructional classes, and so forth; and
- Access to professionals for assistance.

While it is possible to gather data using a questionnaire to ask a representative sample of customers to estimate the value of the service(s) that they used each time they use the library; this, however, can be an expensive proposition. Alternatively, the value of all library services can be (roughly) estimated using a fairly straightforward method, sometimes called the shortcut method. To estimate the value of the library, use the following five-step method:

Step One: Identify all of the services provided by the library and list them in a spreadsheet as shown in table 8.1 for our Example Library.

Step Two: The value of these services may be estimated by identifying a similar competing service in the nearby community for

Table 8.1

Identify Library Service Offerings

SERVICE	LOCAL PRICE (A)	ANNUAL ACTIVITY (B)	ANNUAL BENEFITS (A*B)
Borrowing picture books			
Borrowing adult books			
Video/DVDs			
Audio music/CDs			
Download electronic articles			
Read a magazine			
Read a newspaper			
Reference services—short			
Reference services—long			
Meeting rooms			
Access computer services			
Use of computer software			
Attend a class			
Wi-Fi			
Programs			
Story times			
TOTALS			

which the individual must pay. For example, buying a book at a bookstore would cost, on average, $20, while renting the use of a computer at a commercial establishment might cost $10 per hour. Note that some services may have no economic value assigned to them since similar services are available at no cost within the community; for example, Wi-Fi is available free at the local coffee shop. Table 8.2 shows sample prices for each service.

Table 8.2

Identify Competitor Pricing for Library Service Offerings

SERVICE	LOCAL PRICE (A)	ANNUAL ACTIVITY (B)	ANNUAL BENEFITS (A*B)
Borrowing picture books	$ 8.00		
Borrowing adult books	20.00		
Video/DVDs	4.00		
Audio music/CDs	10.00		
Download electronic articles	15.00		
Read a magazine	2.00		
Read a newspaper	1.00		
Reference services—short	5.00		
Reference services—long	30.00		
Meeting rooms	10.00		
Access computer services	5.00		
Use of computer software	20.00		
Attend a class	15.00		
Wi-Fi	Free		
Programs	Free		
Story times	Free		
TOTALS	n/a		

Step Three: The total volume of transactions for each service is identified and added to the spreadsheet as shown in table 8.3.

Step Four: The total volume of transactions for each service is then multiplied by each price and the value is calculated (multiply column A times column B). These individual values (as table 8.4 indicates) are totaled to determine the total value of library services provided to the university or community.

Table 8.3

Identify Usage of Library Service Offerings (Annual Numbers)

SERVICE	LOCAL PRICE (A)	ANNUAL ACTIVITY (B)	ANNUAL BENEFITS (A*B)
Borrowing picture books	$ 8.00	600,000	
Borrowing adult books	20.00	700,000	
Video/DVDs	4.00	800,000	
Audio music/CDs	10.00	250,000	
Download electronic articles	15.00	1,400,000	
Read a magazine	2.00	12,000	
Read a newspaper	1.00	14,000	
Reference services—short	5.00	124,000	
Reference services—long	30.00	17,000	
Meeting rooms	10.00	63,000	
Access computer services	5.00	845,000	
Use of computer software	20.00	129,000	
Attend a class	15.00	4,800	
Wi-Fi	Free	950,000	
Programs	Free	14,000	
Story times	Free	4,900	
TOTALS	n/a	n/a	

Step Five: The library's annual operating budget is then compared to the estimated value as shown in table 8.5 (divide the total annual benefits by the library's annual operating budget to determine the benefit/cost ratio—which is $4.37 of value [benefits] for every dollar of the library's budget).

One problem that may arise from such an analysis relates to the value of items borrowed from the library's collection. If someone were unable to use the library for some reason, that person might not go to a store and purchase the item. Thus, one study suggested using a value of 15 to 20 percent of the average purchase price for the item being borrowed.[8] Following this advice would lower the calculated ROI.

Table 8.4

Calculate Value of Library Service Offerings

SERVICE	LOCAL PRICE (A)	ANNUAL ACTIVITY (B)	ANNUAL BENEFITS (A*B)
Borrowing picture books	$ 8.00	600,000	$ 4,800,000
Borrowing adult books	20.00	700,000	14,000,000
Video/DVDs	4.00	800,000	3,200,000
Audio music/CDs	10.00	250,000	2,500,000
Download electronic articles	15.00	1,400,000	21,000,000
Read a magazine	2.00	12,000	24,000
Read a newspaper	1.00	14,000	14,000
Reference services—short	5.00	124,000	620,000
Reference services—long	30.00	17,000	510,000
Meeting rooms	10.00	63,000	630,000
Access computer services	5.00	845,000	422,500
Use of computer software	20.00	129,000	2,580,000
Attend a class	15.00	4,800	72,000
Wi-Fi	Free	950,000	0
Programs	Free	14,000	0
Story times	Free	4,900	0
TOTALS	n/a	n/a	$ 50,372,500

The direct economic benefits of library use on a community at large involve two aspects:

1. The economic impact of library spending on salaries, supplies, construction, and other expenditures in the local community that results in additional employment and spending within the community, which has an obvious impact on the local gross domestic product (GDP).

2. Some libraries may be a *destination* due to their unique collections or services that attract people to visit the library, in person or virtually. This destination spending is called the *induced effect* that is indicated by the number of visitors, the amount

Table 8.5

Determine the Cost/Benefit Ratio of Library Service Offerings

SERVICE	LOCAL PRICE (A)	ANNUAL ACTIVITY (B)	ANNUAL BENEFITS (A*B)
Borrowing picture books	$ 8.00	600,000	$ 4,800,000
Borrowing adult books	20.00	700,000	14,000,000
Video/DVDs	4.00	800,000	3,200,000
Audio music/CDs	10.00	250,000	2,500,000
Download electronic articles	15.00	1,400,000	21,000,000
Read a magazine	2.00	12,000	24,000
Read a newspaper	1.00	14,000	14,000
Reference services—short	5.00	124,000	620,000
Reference services—long	30.00	17,000	510,000
Meeting rooms	10.00	63,000	630,000
Access computer services	5.00	845,000	422,500
Use of computer software	20.00	129,000	2,580,000
Attend a class	15.00	4,800	72,000
Wi-Fi	Free	950,000	0
Programs	Free	14,000	0
Story times	Free	4,900	0
TOTALS	n/a	n/a	$50,372,500
LIBRARY BUDGET			$11,530,000
LIBRARY RETURN ON INVESTMENT			$4.37

of visitor spending (influenced by the length of stay), and the size of the multiplier applied to these assumptions. The more visitors, the greater the spending per visitor and the multiplier selected results in a greater economic impact for the library and, in turn, the community.

The *multiplier effect* suggests that the combination of the direct spending plus the induced effect results in additional spending and economic growth within the community. The vast majority of economic impact studies utilize a methodology called multiplier analysis that acknowledges that money spent in the community has a ripple effect that leads to further jobs and additional spending within the community. Depending on the economic model that is used, the multiplier may use a number such as 6, 7, 8, or . . . That is, every dollar spent by the library in the local economy will be increased by the "multiplier," thus resulting in a larger positive economic impact on the community. For many, the concept of the multiplier effect is unrealistic since it is based on restrictive assumptions and has little predictive value.

Perhaps the most widely known economic impact study was prepared for the Seattle Public Library.[9] A survey suggested that as much as 30 percent of the 2.5 million visitors to the library were from out of town. The analysis suggested that these visitors spent $16 million annually in new spending in the downtown Seattle area (hotels, meals, car rentals, parking, ferries, and so forth). A similar economic impact study was prepared for the Carnegie Library of Pittsburgh.[10]

AN ALTERNATIVE APPROACH

An alternative approach in determining the direct benefits from using a library, called the consumer surplus method, is to ask library customers to place a value on their use of the library. Using a survey, the idea is to ask individuals to place a value on a product or service (when this expressed value is in excess of what they paid to get it then the individual has received additional or *surplus* value). While library services are mostly free, customers do pay in the form of time, effort, and direct transportation costs.

Survey respondents are asked, for example, about the number of books they borrow from the public library each year, the number of books purchased annually, and the number of additional books they would buy if they could not borrow from the library. A calculation is then made to determine the value the library user places on borrowing privileges. The same analysis is then prepared for each service offered by the library. The survey approach is expensive, as a fairly large number of respondents must be contacted to ensure accurate results.

INDIRECT BENEFITS

While almost everyone would acknowledge that library customers and the community or university itself benefit from the services provided by a library, it is certainly impossible to calculate all of the economic

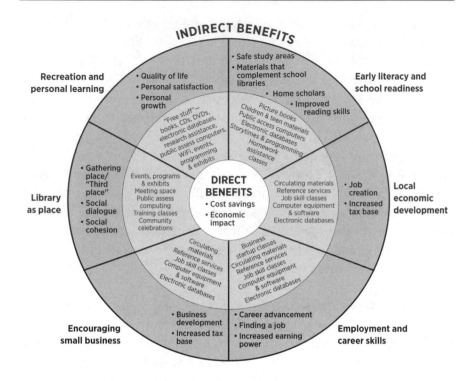

Figure 8.2   Determining the Value of the Public Library

Reprinted from Joseph R. Matthews, "What's the Return on ROI?" *Library Leadership & Management* 25, no. 1 (2011): 8. Reproduced with permission.

benefits. Impossible-to-calculate benefits are known as indirect benefits or public good benefits. Among the wide range of such benefits are leisure enjoyments, literacy encouragement for children and teens, library as place for community meetings, attending a program, and using public access Internet computers (see figure 8.2).

Returning to contingent valuation, it is also a method to calculate indirect benefits. It involves the use of a survey to value nonmarket goods and services. In order to be valid, contingent valuation, either WTP or WTA, integrates valuation motives that extend beyond self-interest but do not violate the assumption of rationality. Ideally, both methods produce similar estimates of benefits. However, WTA usually provides higher benefit estimates since respondents normally include societal or collective benefits in addition to direct benefits. Using WTP, survey respondents state what they would be willing to pay for an improved service, whereas, with WTA, they indicate how much compensation for a decline in service they would be willing to accept. For example, respondents would be asked how much their property taxes would need to be reduced for them to accept the closing of the public library.

Contingent valuation has been applied to numerous cultural studies, particularly when valuing public goods, including assessing the value of national heritage sites, museums, theaters, historical sites, and libraries.[11] Contingent valuation, for instance, was used as part of the process to determine the economic benefits associated, for instance, with the St. Louis Public Library.[12]

Turning to academe, contingent valuation might survey faculty and students about the value of library collections and services. Among the more notable studies are:

- An assessment of library journal collections (physical and electronic) at the University of Pittsburgh. There was an ROI of 2.90:1.[13]
- An analysis connecting citations to resources in the library's collection to successful grant proposals and the resulting grant income. The results at the University of Illinois Urbana-Champaign Library were an ROI of 4.38:1.[14]
- A study of eight other international universities. The ROI for grant-related activities ranged from 27:1 to 15.54:1.[15]
- An analysis of the Bryant University Library that showed the majority of value was associated through the reading of journal articles.[16]
- A study of library use by Carol Tenopir and her colleagues found that the library plays an important role in academic work and success, that downloading of journal articles is critical to scholarly activity, and that successful academics read more (of what the library provides).[17]

The contingent valuation survey technique is not without its detractors. The most frequent problems include:

- Survey respondents may give answers that are inconsistent with the tenets of rational choice;

- Respondents do not always understand what they are being asked to value (respondents generally have no idea of what the current per capita funding for the local public library would be); and
- Many respondents give quick off-the-cuff estimates of value (for example, $25, $50, or . . .). These quick responses may not be truly reflective of a stated value if the person took more time to consider the actual value. Consider, for example, the Marist Institute for Public Opinion, which conducted a national survey using the willingness to pay approach and found that respondents on average were willing to be taxed an additional $49 per year to support public library services.[18] The irony is that the per capita support for public libraries for many thousands of communities across the United States is less than $40.

NONUSE BENEFITS

In addition to use value, economists have recognized that individuals, who make no use of a public good, such as a public library, might derive satisfaction from its mere existence. The literature discussing this concept in the cultural arena has called nonuse value a variety of other names: existence value, bequest value, vicarious consumption, prestige value, education value, and option value, among others.[19] The nonuse value of a library can be considered as the utility individuals obtain from libraries other than their active use of a library. Nonuse value or benefits can be grouped into two categories:

1. It will be a benefit to an individual at some time in the future; and
2. It is of benefit to others in the community now and in the future.

Altruistic motivations, defined as concern for poor people, people of color, children, and others who have access to the broad range of services provided by the public library, are likely to be considered when someone is asked to reflect on the value of public libraries. There is a willingness of individuals to support the library so that others may benefit, and a library is appreciated and valued as an institution that improves the quality of life in the community.

Nonuse benefits are difficult to quantify and if measured are open to considerable debate. While contingent valuation has been used in some studies to determine nonuse benefits, many ROI studies ignore the value of nonuse in an attempt to calculate conservative return on investment numbers.

Total Value

The total value of libraries can be determined, in theory, by combining the use (composed of direct and indirect) and nonuse values. Calculating the total value is problematic since the vast majority of the valuation is based on opinions or estimates from library customers and nonusers within a community, and it ignores the cumulative impact of the library. The cumulative impact is most likely felt in such areas as community development, social inclusiveness, and fostering an open democratic society. A survey of library customers, for instance, found that while it is not possible to show a causal relationship between library use and social capital, there is evidence that such a relationship exists.[20] Interestingly, a large-scale survey in Norway found that citizens are cognizant of the different value components when asked to assess the value of the public library. The survey found about 40 percent of total value is motivated by direct use value, 20 percent by the option for the respondent to use the library in the future, and 40 percent by nonuse value.[21]

And yet, despite the many attempts to place a value on libraries and the services that they provide, the inescapable conclusion is that a library might resist the attempts to quantify its economic value due to significant indirect and nonuse values. Thus, while a library can calculate the direct savings to its customers for their use of the library, there are other perhaps more important components of the value equation that must be part of the conversation about the total value of the library with funding decision makers.

Concluding Thoughts

ROI complements other quantitative and qualitative measures concerning the value of the library so that library managers can provide evidence to stakeholders while trying to sustain support and funding in the future. Relying on a single measure, such as ROI, is not likely to produce a positive reaction among the library's funding decision makers year after year. As most library directors know, no silver bullet leads to sustained library funding. Still, it is important to view ROI but as one of several key performance measures.

Exercises

1. You have been asked to prepare an ROI analysis for your library. The first step is to identify what competitors exist within your community as well as the cost to use a specific service. Use the service offerings as shown in table 8.2 to identify a competitor and the local cost for each service offering.

2. Prepare an ROI analysis for your library by following the steps laid out earlier in this chapter. Make sure that you have a relatively complete list of service offerings, carefully consider possible competitors (located within your community and online), identify the competitor's price for each service, determine the annual amount of use for each service, and calculate the annual value of each service offering. Finally, determine the total annual value of the benefits of using the library and its services and then finally calculate the benefit to cost ratio (also called the return on investment—ROI).

   Does your library's ROI fall in the typical 4:1 to 6:1 ratio for other libraries that have completed an ROI study? If not, what would you attribute your higher (or lower) ROI value rating to?

3. Look at the benefit values found in table 8.5 and reflect on the fact that more than three-fourths of the total benefit value for library services comes from downloading electronic resources and borrowing library materials. Would you estimate that three-fourths of the library's budget is spent on providing these services? Is there an imbalance between the resources needed to provide services that are used less and thus contribute a small amount of annual value? Does this raise any concerns?

4. Increase (or decrease) the value assigned to the download-ing of e-resources and the borrowing of materials by 25 per-cent or 40 percent. What impact does this have on the result-ing recalculated ROI? (The idea with this exercise is that you will begin to develop an appreciation for the impact that the assigned value has on the final ROI calculation.)

(Answers to these questions are in the "Appendix" at the back of the book. We encourage different members of a library staff to work on the exercises together and to discuss the results.)

NOTES

1. A. R. Prest and R. Turvey, "Cost/Benefit Analysis: A Survey," *Economic Journal* 75, no. 300 (December 1965): 683–735.

2. Association of College and Research Libraries, *Value of Academic Libraries: A Comprehensive Research Review and Report*, prepared by Megan Oakleaf (Chicago: Association of College and Research Libraries, 2010), 73.

3. Ibid., 74.

4. Christine Urquhart, "How Do I Measure the Impact of My Service?" in *Evidence-Based Practice for Information Professionals: A Handbook*, ed. Andrew Booth and Anne Brice (London: Facet, 2004), 212.

5. Association of College and Research Libraries, *Value of Academic Libraries*, 77.

6. Examples of public library websites that provide a library use value calculator include Maine State Library (www.maine.gov/msl/services/calculator.htm), the Chelmsford Library (www.chelmsfordlibrary.org/library_info/calculator.html), the Lansing Public Library (www.lansing .lib.il.us/value.html), and the Henderson County Public Library (www .hcpl.org/library/value.html). For academic libraries, there is the University of West Florida Libraries: student ROI, http://libguides .uwf.edu/content.php?pid = 188487&sid = 2183215; personal ROI, http://libguides.uwf.edu/content.php?pid = 188487&sid = 2261667; and institutional ROI, http://libguides.uwf.edu/content.php?pid = 188487&sid = 2184200.

7. Tefko Saracevic and Paul Kantor, "Studying the Value of Library and In-formation Services: Part I, Establishing the Theoretical Framework," *Journal of the American Society of Information Science* 48, no. 6 (1997): 527–42; and Tefko Saracevic and Paul Kantor, "Studying the Value of Library and Information Services: Part II, Methodology and Taxonomy," *Journal of the American Society of Information Science* 48, no. 6 (1997): 543–63.

8. John Sumsion, Margaret Hawkins, and Anne Morris, "Estimating the Economic Value of Library Benefits," *Performance Measurement and Metrics* 4, no. 1 (2003): 13–27.

9. Berk & Associates, *The Seattle Public Library Central Library: Economic Benefits Assessment: The Transformative Power of a Library to Redefine Learning, Community, and Economic Development* (Seattle, WA: Berk & Associates, 2005), www.berkandassociates.com/pdf/DraftReport.pdf.

10. Carnegie Mellon University, *Carnegie Library of Pittsburgh: Community Impact and Benefits* (Pittsburgh, PA: Carnegie Mellon University, Center for Economic Development, 2006).

11. Doug Noonan, *Contingent Valuation Studies in the Arts and Culture: An Annotated Bibliography* (Chicago: University of Chicago, Cultural Policy Center, 2002), http://culturalpolicy.uchicago.edu/papers/workingpapers/ Noonan11.pdf.

12. Donald S. Elliott, Glen E. Holt, Sterling W. Hayden, and Leslie Edmonds Holt, *Measuring Your Library's Value: How to Do a Cost-Benefit Analysis for Your Public Library* (Chicago: American Library Association, 2007).

13. Donald King, Sarah Aerni, Fern Brody, Matt Habison, and Amy Knapp, *The Use and Outcomes of University Library Print and Electronic Collections* (Pittsburgh, PA: Sara Fine Institute for Interpersonal Behavior and Technology, 2004); Saint Louis Public Library, "Public Library Benefits Valuation Study: Key Findings," www.slpl.lib.mo.us/libsrc/valuationg.htm.

14. Judy Luther, "University Investment in the Library: What's the Return? A Case Study at the University of Illinois at Urbana-Champaign," *Library Connect* (Elsevier, 2008). See also Paula Kaufman and Sarah Barbara Watstein, "Library Value (Return on Investment, ROI) and the Challenge of Placing a Value on Public Services," *Reference Services Review* 36, no. 3 (2008): 226–31.

15. Carol Tenopir, Amy Love, Joseph Park, Lei Wu, Bruce Kigma, and Donald King. "Return on Investment in Academic Libraries: An International Study of the Value of Research Libraries to the Grants Process," *Library Connect* (Elsevier, 2009).

16. Donald King, "Demonstration of Methods to Assess the Use, Value, and ROI of All Academic Library Services" (2012), available from http:// libvalue.cci.utk.edu/content/lib-value-publications-presentations-reports.

17. Carol Tenopir, Regina Mays, and Lei Wu, "Journal Article Growth and Reading Patterns," *New Review of Information Networking* 16 (2011): 4–22.

18. Lee Miringoff, "The Public Library: A National Survey" (Poughkeepsie, NY: The Marist College Institute for Public Opinion, 2003). A PowerPoint

presentation of the poll's results is available at http://midhudson.org/funding/advocacy/Marist_Poll_2003.ppt.

19. Svanhild Aabø, "Value of Public Libraries," in *New Frontiers in Public Library Research*, ed. Carl Johannsen and Leif Kajbrg (Lanham, MD: Scarecrow, 2005), 97–109.

20. Catherine A Johnson, "Do Public Libraries Contribute to Social Capital? A Preliminary Investigation into the Relationship," *Library & Information Science Research* 32, no. 2 (2010): 147–55.

21. Svanhild Aabø and Jon Strand, "Public Library Valuation, Nonuse Values, and Altruistic Motivations," *Library & Information Science Research* 26, no. 3 (2004): 351–72.

9

MEASURING THE VALUE OF THE LIBRARY AND ITS SERVICES

The primary challenge for a library is to determine the value for the customer to use library services, both physically and virtually. Those using the library therefore assign value and so do those not using the library. Naturally there is a difference in the value assigned by each group; one assigns a positive value and the other probably assigns no value. Broadly speaking, value is a form of outcome, the impact of the library in the life of its customer as the customer makes the assignment of value.

Framework for Establishing Value

Tefko Saracevic and Paul Kantor developed a framework or taxonomy for establishing the impact that a library or information service has directly on the individual and indirectly on the organization.[1] These impacts can be grouped into six categories:

Cognitive results. Use of the library may have an impact on the mind of the individual. The intent of this category is to ask the question, "What was learned?" Thus, the customer may have:

- Refreshed memory of detail or facts
- Substantiated or reinforced knowledge or belief
- Provided new knowledge
- Change in viewpoint, outlook, or perspective
- Getting ideas with a slightly different or tangential perspective (serendipity)
- Getting no ideas

Affective results. Use of the library or its services may influence or have an emotional impact on the individual. The customer may experience:

- A sense of accomplishment, success, or satisfaction
- A sense of confidence, reliability, and trust
- A sense of comfort, happiness, and good feelings
- A sense of failure
- A sense of frustration

Meeting expectations. When using the library or an information service, the individual may:

- Be getting what he or she needed, sought, or expected
- Getting too much
- Getting nothing
- Have confidence in what he or she received
- Receive more than expected
- Seek substitute sources or action if what he or she received did not meet expectations

Accomplishments in relation to tasks. As a result of using the library, the individual is able to:

- Make better informed decisions
- Achieve a higher quality performance
- Point to a course of action
- Proceed to the next step
- Discover people and/or other sources of information
- Improve a policy, procedure, and plan

Time aspects. Some of the real value for the customer of a library is the fact that the information provided might lead to the savings of time in several possible ways. The individual may:

- Save time as a result of using the service
- Waste time as a result of using the service
- Need to wait for service
- Experience a service that ranges from slow to fast
- Need time to understand how to use a service or resource

Money aspects. Using the library or information service may, in some cases, clearly result in saving money or generating new revenues. The individual may be able to provide an:

- Estimate of the dollar value of results obtained from a service or information received
- Estimate of the amount of money saved due to the use of the service
- Estimate of the cost in using the service
- Estimate of what may be spent on a substitute service
- Estimate of value (in dollars) lost where the service was not available or use was not successful

Identifying the value of the academic library is challenging, as Megan Oakleaf demonstrated.[2] She suggested that library value could be demonstrated in three broad areas: student-related metrics, faculty productivity, and institutional prestige (see box 9.1). Complicating matters, libraries are not perceived as playing a role, at least a meaningful one, with some of the metrics, namely graduation rate and affordability of a degree. Graduation rate and retention rate involve more than the analysis of typical library inputs and include satisfaction (an output) and mastery of learning goals (outcomes).

When collecting evidence about the value of the public library to the community and its impact on people's lives, four primary roles can be examined and reported:

1. **Traditional function:** reading and literacy, providing access to information, leisure reading, and education
2. **Social and caring role:** including personal development, community empowerment and learning, local image, and social cohesion

Box 9.1

Oakleaf's Areas of Academic Library Value and Potential Surrogates

Student-Related

STUDENT ENROLLMENT

- Recruitment of potential students
- Matriculation of admitted students
- Recommendation of current students

STUDENT LEARNING

- Learning assessment
- Faculty judgment

STUDENT ACHIEVEMENT

- GPA
- Professional/educational test scores

STUDENT RETENTION

- Fall-to-fall retention
- Graduation rates

STUDENT EXPERIENCES

- Engagement surveys
- Senior/alumni surveys
- Help surveys
- Alumni donations

STUDENT SUCCESS

- Internship success
- Job placement
- Job salaries
- Professional/graduate school acceptance
- Marketable skills

Faculty-Related

RESEARCH PRODUCTIVITY

- Number of patents, value of technology transfer
- Number of publications
- Tenure/promotion judgments

FACULTY GRANTS

- Number of grant proposals (funded or unfunded)
- Value of grants funded

FACULTY TEACHING

- Integration of library resources
- Faculty/librarian collaborations

General

INSTITUTIONAL PRESTIGE

- Faculty recruitment
- Institutional rankings
- Community engagement

Association of College and Research Libraries, *The Value of Academic Libraries: A Comprehensive Research Review and Report,* prepared by Megan Oakleaf (Chicago: Association of College and Research Libraries, 2010). Reproduced with permission.

3. **Equity** between groups and communities as well as equity of access
4. **Economic impact:** including business and employment information, training opportunities, and tourism information

Figure 9.1 summarizes the various approaches to identify the value of a public library. These approaches can be divided into two broad groups: economic and social. The social category encompasses a broad variety of topics in which the library makes an impact. For example, in academe, what is the impact of library services on student learning, student retention, and student enrollment? In a public library, stakeholders might be interested in the library's contribution to children's reading levels, improving reading skills as a result of participation in a summer reading program, the library's efforts to encourage entrepreneurs in starting businesses within the community, and so forth.

Of course, the problems of attempting to assess outcomes are complicated by the fact that the benefits from the use of the library may accrue directly to the individual user, indirectly to the community, or both. In

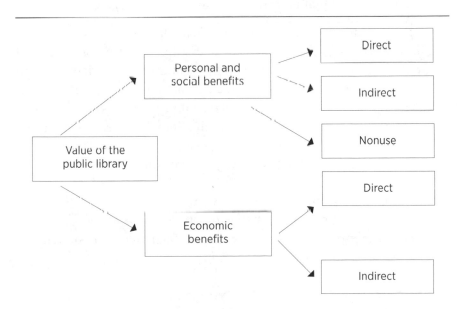

Figure 9.1   Categories of Possible Public Library Benefits

addition to the traditional use of input, process, and output measures, some have attempted to identify either the social benefits or economic benefits that occur as the result of using the library. Yet, there are problems associated with the measurement of these benefits.

Value of Public Libraries

Generally, it is possible to separate the possible economic benefits that arise from a public library into two categories: direct and indirect benefits. A library can identify economic benefits using four different methodologies:[3]

- Cost-benefit analysis (discussed in greater detail in chapter 8);
- Economic impact, the contribution of actual dollars to the local community by the library (also discussed in greater detail in chapter 8);
- Subsidies the public library provides through its services to other organizations in the community; and
- Cost avoidance; a service provided by the public library need not be duplicated by other private or government agencies.

Generally, unless otherwise noted below, data about the impact of the library will be gathered using a survey (paper-based or online) of library customers. The assumption is that library stakeholders are willing to rely on self-reported evidence about impact. The challenge is to ensure that a representative sample of library customers is included (data are gathered during all hours that the library is open). In addition, it is important that a fairly large sample size is achieved in order to be able to report the results with any degree of confidence in them.

DIRECT BENEFITS FOR THE INDIVIDUAL, LOCAL BUSINESSES, AND THE COMMUNITY

Chapter 8 discusses possible direct economic benefits for an individual, local businesses, and the local community.

INDIRECT BENEFITS FOR THE INDIVIDUAL

Stephen Krashen has suggested that with the more free voluntary reading that is done by an individual, there are a number of striking improvements in a number of intellectual skills, including reading comprehension, writing style, vocabulary, and spelling.[4] According to him, the benefit of direct instruction in the classroom rewards readers and sets up nonreaders for failure.

A library interested in determining the effects of its summer reading program could partner with local schools to gather and analyze the impact of the extent of participation. The schools might provide reading test scores or have the teachers assess the students' reading ability at the end of the school year and the start of the next school year.[5]

Reading has such extraordinary benefits while capturing a child's imagination. The child's ability to read improves while at the same time the child learns to think, and how to write better. The mere existence of a public library causes children who live nearby to read more, and the library can encourage more parent/child interaction by encouraging them to read together every day.

INDIRECT BENEFITS FOR LOCAL BUSINESS

Possible indirect economic benefits for the local community include the following:

- Literate workforce
- Workforce trained in using current information technology
- A population that is happy with their lives and where they live

Employers are seeking potential employees that are literate and motivated. In some cases, the availability of a wide range of reading materials promotes the goal of supporting "lifelong learning" among the citizens of a community. Given the rapid rate of change in our society in general and with technology in particular, it is important for people to upgrade their skills so that they can remain competitive in the marketplace. It is not surprising that a number of residents will turn to the public library for information resources as they pursue their goals of learning.

INDIRECT BENEFITS FOR THE LOCAL COMMUNITY

While some quality of life indexes (*best places to live*, *best places to retire*, and so forth) use a *books per capita* statistic as one factor among many when rating communities, the reality is that a good-quality public library has only a modest impact on the overall rating of a community.

Other factors such as crime, recreational opportunities, weather, health, and the environment are much more important in the quality of life ratings, which are often "weighted" to reflect higher values.

Examples from the Literature

Using the library's integrated library system (ILS), it is a fairly straightforward task to determine who is actually using the library's collections (if in-library use is ignored for a moment). An analysis can be prepared that identifies each unique individual, the number of times the collection was used, and the number of items borrowed. Such data are then combined with other data obtained from the registrar's office or the office of institutional research.[6] For example, partnering with the University's Office of Institutional Research, librarians at the University of Minnesota Libraries measured how often, and in what ways, students used library services. The team investigated ways to match library service usage to individual accounts while retaining patron privacy to determine who was and was not using the library. With complete data sets, the group was able to determine overall usage rates for undergraduate and graduate students and compare how students in different colleges used library services.

The University of Minnesota team also examined the impact library usage has on the retention and academic success of first-time, first-year undergraduate students at a large, public research university. Usage statistics were gathered during the fall 2011 semester for thirteen library access points. Analysis of the data suggests first-time, first-year undergraduate students who use the library have a higher GPA for their first semester and higher retention from fall to spring than nonlibrary users.[7]

While libraries easily can obtain transaction data about who is borrowing materials or downloading articles online, it is clear that the majority of academic libraries do not routinely gather the unique individual identification number of each person who uses reference services, attends information literacy training sessions, and so forth. Yet, if library managers want to determine the actual impact of the library's services, they will need to obtain such data while addressing individual privacy concerns.

Oakleaf notes examples of academic libraries that have estimated their monetary value. For instance, Cornell University librarians estimated the library value at $90,648,785 in 2008/2009. However, they did not attempt to place a monetary value on some electronic collections, public computers, library instruction, and some special collections. She, however, concludes that "large-scale valuation studies are challenging and may not be feasible for all libraries," even if other libraries replicate the process.[8] For this reason, before a library engages in determining value, its managers should review the Cornell University Library's (CUL) web page on "library value calculations," which notes:

> We all know that maintaining a research library requires a large investment. The annual expenditure figures of a library quantify the investment, but do not tell the whole story How do we quantify the other side of the story, the contributions the library makes in return to the university? Research libraries are not used to assigning a monetary value to the use of their collections, services and expertise, although public libraries have been moving into this direction in the past few years. . . . The bottom line: . . . we generate more value than how much money is expended on supporting our operations.[9]

Such evaluations enable users to see the personal value they gain but also cost data on what an institution would face if it did not have a library. Value to the institution is important to consider in these times when administrators may assume that everything is available for free on the Internet and, therefore, question the existence of a library. Cornell's library focused on the following categories:

- the use of physical volumes
- articles accessed online and through interlibrary services
- answering questions to build research skills and contribute to Cornell research results
- in-depth consultations that contribute to Cornell research results
- use of preprints from arXiv.org

- distributing Cornell-created content to the world through eCommons
- laptops borrowed

For each category, the web page shows how the total cost was determined.[10] Thus, other libraries might use the same categories, alter the categories, or pick select ones to examine and share with institutional administrators. However, part of the institutional value might be the social impact of libraries on students; social impact is also relevant to public libraries.[11]

Outlining a Process for Getting Started

A number of issues must be addressed as a library develops an action plan. First, decide what is important to campus decision makers or community stakeholders. Examine the organization's mission and vision statements and review the latest strategic plan. In an academic environment, retaining students or improving the number of graduates might be an important goal. Some public libraries have focused on education by improving existing programs and services for early childhood reading as well as developing new programs. The library might also explore programs for providing GED classes or matching tutors to those interested in improving their English skills.

Second, determine whether the data that the library currently collects about individual users can be combined with other institutional data in order to analyze the library's impact on its customers. In some cases, it may be necessary to identify new data that must be collected in order to prepare the desired analysis.

Third, determine what other institutional departments and units the library might partner with in order to gain access to needed data and to produce an analysis that will be of high quality. Partnering with others will improve the credibility of the resulting analysis, and more talented people with other skills will likely be involved in the project.

Fourth, be prepared to produce a written report documenting the data collection and analysis process that also clearly identifies the conclusions that can be drawn from the analysis. It is also important to identify the limitations of the data analysis. And, finally, be prepared to communicate the results of the analysis to all stakeholders, library staff members, and library customers in a variety of ways—all of which will capture their attention.

Concluding Thoughts

Based on the previous section, as part of its action plan, a library should consider the placement of a calculator on its home page so that students and their parents (academic library) or the public and stakeholders (public library) can make their only calculations. Chapter 8 introduces calculations for determining ROI and notes that a number of libraries use them. It is possible to replicate such calculators,[12] place them in a prominent place on the library's website, and monitor the number of hits. Further, who uses them and for what purposes?

The Massachusetts Library Association has a widely used and adapted library value calculator. A web page shows the sources upon which value is determined. Thus, although values are dated, managers can easily update those values provided.[13] The Pasadena Public Library (California), for instance, has one that asks "How much would you have to pay out-of-pocket for the library services that are provided for free?" and then lets the user calculate the "Total Monthly Value of your library use" based on seventeen items.[14]

If a library wants to engage in a valuation study (and we recommend that it should), it should first determine what items to monitor on a recurring basis and then ensure that relevant data are regularly captured and reported. In so doing it could produce annual trend charts instead of conducting a valuation study on an irregular basis. Which of the following are most important to the library and its institution and broader organization? The list from which to select might include:[15]

    ____ books were borrowed, which would have cost users $_____

    ____ DVDs and videos were borrowed, which would have
         cost users $_____

    ____ e-books were borrowed, which would have cost users $_____

    ____ books were used in the library, which would have
         cost users $_____

_____ magazines, journals, and newspapers were used in the
library, which would have cost users $_____

_____ uses of e-reserves system, if photocopied, would have
cost users $_____

_____ articles were downloaded from full-text databases,
which would have cost users $_____

_____ reference questions were answered at library service
points, which would have cost users $_____

_____ research consultations provided by librarians would
have cost users $_____

_____ library and information competence instruction sessions
were presented, which would have cost users $_____

_____ online library tutorials and guides were prepared
for discipline and classroom use, which would have
cost users $_____

_____ log-ins of library workstations would have cost users $_____

_____ laptops were borrowed, which would have cost users $_____

_____ filled interlibrary borrowing and lending requests would
have cost users $_____

Exercises

1. Review the list of categories highlighted in "Concluding Thoughts." What would you add, delete, and which are most relevant to your library?

2. Which of those selected would be most relevant to institutional leaders?

3. Are there any indicators related to social impact that you would include? Why?

4. For the list of preferred categories, how would you calculate the cost? Be sure to address the evidence on which you would rely.

5. Use one of the calculators discussed in this chapter or in chapter 8. Use the results to write a story that would attract readers of a local newspaper or campus newspaper. Ask others—not all librarians—to review the article for potential community impact.

(Answers to these questions are in the "Appendix" at the back of the book. We encourage different members of a library staff to work on the exercises together and to discuss the results.)

NOTES

1. Tefko Saracevic and Paul B. Kantor, "Studying the Value of Library and Information Services: Part I, Establishing a Theoretical Framework," *Journal of the American Society of Information Science* 48, no. 6 (1997): 527–42; and Tefko Saracevic and Paul B. Kantor, "Studying the Value of Library and Information Services: Part II, Methodology and Taxonomy," *Journal of the American Society of Information Science* 48, no. 6 (1997): 543–63.

2. Association of College and Research Libraries, *The Value of Academic Libraries: A Comprehensive Research Review and Report*, prepared by Megan Oakleaf (Chicago: Association of College and Research Libraries, 2010).

3. Jennifer Abend and Charles R. McClure, "Recent Views on Identifying Impacts from Public Libraries," *Public Library Quarterly* 17, no. 3 (1999): 3–29.

4. Stephen Krashen, *The Power of Reading* (Westport, CT: Libraries Unlimited, 2004).

5. Joseph Matthews, "Evaluating Summer Reading Programs: Suggested Improvements," *Public Libraries* 49, no. 4 (July/August 2010): 34–39.

6. Joseph Matthews, "Assessing Library Contributions to University Outcomes: The Need for Individual Student Level Data," *Library Management* 33, nos. 6/7 (2012): 389–402.

7. Shane Nackerud, Jan Fransen, Kate Peterson, and Kristen Mastel, "Analyzing Demographics: Assessing Library Use across the Institution," *portal: Libraries and the Academy* 13, no. 2 (April 2013): 131–45. See also Krista Soria, Jan Fransen, and Shane Nackeru, "Library Use

and Undergraduate Student Outcomes: New Evidence for Students' Retention and Academic Success," *portal: Libraries and the Academy* 13, no. 2 (April 2013): 147–64.

8. Association of College and Research Libraries, *The Value of Academic Libraries*, 49.

9. Cornell University Library, Research & Assessment Unit, "Library Value Calculations" (n.d.), http://research.library.cornell.edu/value.

10. Ibid.

11. Association of College and Research Libraries, *The Value of Academic Libraries,* 79–81.

12. Maine State Library, "Library Use Value Calculator" (2011), www.maine .gov/msl/services/calculator.htm; and Maine State Library, "Customization of the Library Use Value Calculator" (n.d.), www.maine.gov/msl/ services/customcal.htm.

13. Massachusetts Library Association, "Value of Library Service Calculator" (n.d.), www.masslib.org/value-new/calculator.html; and Massachusetts Library Association, "How Those Values Were Calculated" (2008), www .masslib.org/value-new/how.html.

14. City of Pasadena, Pasadena Public Library, "What Is Your Library Worth?" (2013), www.ci.pasadena.ca.us/library/about_the_library/ value_calculator/.

15. A number of the categories were derived from California State University -Northridge, Oviat Library, "Assessment" (2008), http://library.csun.edu/ About/Assessment.

10

USING AND
COMMUNICATING
THE RESULTS

Almost all evaluation efforts are designed to assist library managers in making improvements to their services so that they are more responsive to their customers' needs and expectations. In some cases, evaluation activities might be designed to improve a library's internal operations by making them more efficient and cost-effective. However, if all of these evaluation efforts are hidden, a library loses a wonderful opportunity to communicate with interested stakeholders.

Effectively communicating the benefits of library services is perhaps as important as managing a well-run library. Developing a communications strategy or plan identifies the ways to communicate the value of the library to stakeholders. From the perspective of the stakeholder, being presented with numerous facts and figures does not communicate the impact that the library has on individuals and on the community itself.

Aside from communicating evaluation results to make improvements and to communicate the benefits that arise from the use of the library, libraries often communicate findings for advocacy purposes. That is, the intent is to inform potential donors and partners about the library and its impact. This is admittedly a self-serving purpose in that it may lead to a broadening of the financial base for the library as well as assist a partner with achieving its own goals and objectives. Another communication benefit is that the library may gain increased visibility in the form of improved public relations or promotion efforts.

Once the library has gathered and analyzed data, and reached some conclusions, it needs to answer several questions pertaining to whom it communicates, why, and when.

To Whom Do We Communicate?

It is obvious that a broad array of individuals might be interested in the library's evaluation efforts. Among these are:

Library staff members. Staff want to know how the results will be used because their job responsibilities might be changing (perhaps in a big way). The library's leadership team must clearly and consistently communicate its intentions about an evaluation project from the time the project is conceived. In almost all cases, an evaluation report is prepared that documents the intent of the project and why a particular methodology was chosen, discusses the data collected and the results of the evaluation, and presents the conclusions drawn.

Friends groups. Members of library Friends groups like to know that the time they volunteer to raise funds for the library through book sales and other activities is appreciated. One way, in addition to an annual event to acknowledge their contributions, is to demonstrate that the library is a good steward of the monies provided to the library.

Prospective donors. Donors that are potentially interested in making a sizable gift to the library are interested in how their donation will impact library users. While in past times the idea of giving to the library was fairly easy to justify as the library was, for instance, the heart of the university, now donors are interested in the real short-term and long-term outcomes that result from using the library.

Board of trustees. Any library board is interested in the success of the library. Historically libraries have presented output metrics as a surrogate for the value and goodness of the library. And, while use of the library is one measure, libraries need to identify how use impacts the life of the customer in some (hopefully positive) manner. Thus, libraries need to demonstrate the value of the library using outcome metrics.

Community governing boards. For a public library, the community governing board is the mayor, city council members, city manager, county board of supervisors, county administrative officer, and so forth.

Institutional stakeholders. For an academic library the institutional stakeholders are a number of influential individuals such as the chancellor, president, provost, deans, and department heads. This group wants to know about the value of the library in terms that matter to the college or university. An academic campus might be interested in student success metrics such as grade point average and time-to-degree. Other campuses might focus institutional resources on improving student retention, and so forth, especially in these times of demands for increasing accountability. Funding decision makers for the library are the principal audience for the message concerning the value of the library. These individuals want to know that the library uses those resources in a responsible and cost-efficient manner and that the community values and appreciates library services.

Library administrative agencies. Every library typically reports a series of performance metrics to a number of local, state, or national organizations. Some of this reporting is mandated and some is optional; many libraries report these metrics every year to several agencies. Among them are state legislatures, the state library, professional library associations, and federal agencies. The value for each library reporting its statistics and performance metrics is that they contribute to a large data set from which a library can draw for comparative and other purposes.

State legislatures. Many state legislatures have historically provided a large portion of state college and university budgets, although the percentage of a university's budget received from a state has been declining in recent years. Most state legislatures require some kind of annual report of performance metrics so that they can get some kind of sense of their return on investment.

Customers. The library's customers may also be interested in knowing more about the impact of the library in the lives of other customers. Historically some libraries have developed annual reports where use data are typically provided and discussed. However, most library annual reports are dry and provide data in ways that are not engaging and do not use the language of the customer. Not many people know or can comprehend the implications of what annual circulation actually means. For academic libraries it may be necessary to develop messages depending on the specific group of library customers to be addressed. Among the more important customer groups on campus are:

- **Faculty.** In general, faculty members rely less on the library's physical collections and more on the electronic resources the library provides. The important role that the library plays in providing access to these expensive resources needs to be periodically highlighted for the faculty.
- **Graduate students.** Students involved in graduate work need to have access to both electronic resources and physical collections. They are often unaware of their inability to find and use high-quality resources (even if they think they are doing a good job already).
- **Undergraduate students.** These students often use the library more as a study space and a place to meet friends and to gain access to information technology resources rather than use library collections and services. Yet, it is still important to have a clear message about how the library can help them succeed in their educational endeavors.

What Do We Communicate?

It is important to develop relationships with stakeholders and funding decision makers so that library managers understand how they prefer to receive information. Some people are auditory learners, some visual (graphic) learners, and still others prefer to read textual material. It is important to visit with them on their turf and learn what their current problems and priorities are in order to determine if the library can provide information that will be of value.

The content of the message (e.g., report or document) should tell an important, interesting part of the library's story. The choice of performance metrics that reflect the benefits of library services is obviously critical. The selection of these metrics must be made with the understanding that the resulting information is relevant to local decision makers. In addition, the information being communicated to these stakeholders must be understandable to nonlibrarians. The text should explain how the findings answer the question(s) that formed the purpose of the evaluation, make clear the implications of the results, ensure that the recommendations are explicit, and offer strategies for how the recommendations can be implemented. The information being communicated must be free of library jargon and acronyms. Talking about "circulation per capita," for instance, means little to most stakeholders.

How Do We Communicate?

Libraries have reported findings for years, typically to support accountability related to funding and library operations, including input and output metrics in such areas as collection development, expenditures, staffing, resource usage, and program or event attendance. Librarians can choose a wide variety of ways and techniques with which to communicate information to stakeholders. Among the more popular approaches are text reports, graphs, or PowerPoint presentations, one page or a tri-fold flyer, a statistical report with some discussion of the reported measures, video, annual report, one or more pages on a website, and so forth. The choice of the approach depends on the individuals or group to whom the information is being provided. There may be several versions of the findings, each geared to meet the needs of specific and diverse stakeholders, presented formally or informally, in oral or written form, and in combinations of these means as appropriate for the content and audience.

Effective communication occurs when the choice of medium being used to communicate the message is appropriate for the intended audience, as shown in figure 10.1. Having a clear goal of the message or messages that the library wants to communicate is the foundation upon which all communication about the value of the library rests.

Text is the most common form for the presentation of library findings, and it may be supplemented with tables, charts, and graphs. Tables

Rich Channels	One-on-One / Face-to-Face Communications
	Hallway / Coffeepot Communications
	Small Group Meetings
	Video Communications
	Telephone Conversations
	Voice Mail
	E-mail
	Large Group Meetings
	Handwritten Personal Notes
	Copies of Meeting Agendas
	Faxes
	Memos
	Formal Speeches
	Letters
	Newsletters
Lean Channels	Reports

Figure 10.1   Communication Continuum

Adapted from: Joseph M. Miniace and Elizabeth Falter, "Communication: A Key Factor in Strategy Implementation," *Strategy & Leadership,* 24, no. 1 (January–February 1996): 29. Reprinted with permission.

present numerical information more efficiently than can be expressed in text. A best practice is if a paragraph has more than five numbers, a table should be considered.[1] A table conveys the most important ideas about the data through the table's title and the labeling of the rows and columns.

Data in raw form tell no story; presenting information in graphic form can, in many cases, be a much more effective way to communicate the library's message. For example, a chart can provide a visual display that conveys content that would not be readily apparent if data were displayed in a table or as text. However, care must be exercised in the use of graphics because the availability of such programs as PowerPoint has made such graphical presentations routine and often humdrum. Some suggestions for improving the use of graphical presentations include:

- Make the number of graphics quite small;
- Make sure the graphic can stand on its own and minimize text;
- A simple (and memorable) graphic is preferred over the complex; and
- Test each graphic. Make sure it is communicating the message intended.[2]

Remember that the color of graphics and other images can have an impact. The warmer colors (yellow, orange, and red) convey energy, enthusiasm, warmth, and even danger. The color green conveys feelings of growth and optimism, while the color blue imparts feelings of trust and loyalty.

Raw statistical data have little meaning to those the library is trying to impress. Providing some context or comparison about what a particular statistical measure means significantly improves the communication process. Whether showing trends over time, appropriate comparisons, or references to established standards, context translates a simple number into a persuasive story. Mentioning that "circulation per capita" is among the highest 10 percent in the state for comparable libraries has greater meaning than the raw number itself. Comparing the weekly or monthly attendance at the public library to attendance at sporting events or the local movie theater may provide a more meaningful impression about how frequently the library is used. Develop zippy one-liners such as "public library services for 'x' cents per day per citizen," or "we provide library services for 'y' cents per use," or "the entire population of 'your city' visits the library every 'z' days!"

Written reports may include charts, graphs, and other visuals, but those preparing the reports need to make it easier for readers to understand relationships between data points. The appropriate type of chart or graph should be used so as to stand alone, leading the reader to understand the context with its title and axis titles, and data points. Commonly found charts include pie, bar, time series, and scatterplots:[3]

> **Pie charts** are a popular way of showing proportions, often using percentages encoded as slices of the pie. They must include the whole to which the represented proportional pieces combine for the 100 percent of the graphic. For clarity, one should avoid displaying three-dimensional pie charts and two pie charts side-by-side for comparison.
>
> **Bar charts** display the relationship between one or more categorical variables with one or more quantitative variables, usually frequency, represented by the length and height of the bars. Each column represents a group defined by a categorical variable in a simple bar chart. A commonly used variation of the bar chart is the stacked bar chart, which is a method for visualizing change in a set of items, where the sum of the values is as important as the individual items. Another variation is the histogram, which is used to display a frequency distribution of a continuous variable along a set of defined categorical ranges. A histogram displays the distribution of numeric values in a data set. Its X-axis is divided into bins that correspond to value ranges. Each item in the data set is drawn as a rectangular block, and the blocks are piled into the bins to show how many values exist in each range.
>
> **A time series chart** is an efficient method for displaying data to visualize continuous change. Usually time is displayed on the X-axis from left to right, and multiple lines can be displayed on a single time series chart, which facilitates comparisons.
>
> **Scatterplots are two-dimensional charts** and are used to show relationships between two continuous or interval-level variables (use the mean as the average) more simply than any other method of

presenting data. A specific type of scatterplot is a quadrant, which is a useful tool for librarians in three ways: visual analysis and presentation, decision making, and impact analysis. A quadrant chart might be used, for example, to visualize current user perceptions, identify and visualize a gap between user and staff perceptions, aid decision making regarding resource allocation, identify actionable strategic options that are framed by research results (the survey and resultant user perceptions as plotted on the quadrant), and visualize positive and negative impacts to understand better related benefits as libraries apply resources to affect outcomes in a continuous effort to improve service for users.

In some cases, especially for larger public libraries, providing statistical information in map format has real appeal since this is something that local stakeholders see on a fairly frequent basis. It is relatively easy to import data into a geographical information system and produce some striking maps revealing library use across the jurisdiction.

An increasingly popular visual display is a dashboard, which is a visual representation of key performance indicators that give the viewer a snapshot on how a selected objective is performing against a standard or benchmark. One example is the "Accountability Dashboard" of the Minnesota State Colleges and Universities, which monitors the performance of the state system on selected key measures. Designed "as a tool for the Board of Trustees, institutions, policymakers and other visitors," it provides "information to improve . . . services to students and to the citizens of [the state]." Results are shown for the system as whole, separately for four-year universities and two-year colleges, and for each institution. Students and parents will want to check other information in websites and publications created to help make decisions about attending higher education.[4]

Another popular visualization is a word cloud, which displays the frequency of a word in a text. The size of a word in the cloud is proportional to the quantity associated with that word, which, in the case of free text, is the word count. A word cloud can be useful when reviewing the relative frequency of word occurrences in a text. It may be that, based upon the visual frequency, the words that are emphasized (appear larger than others) are, or are not, the words the writer wants to emphasize. When used with recorded feedback from library users, the cloud might be helpful to raise awareness of what is most frequently associated with the library.

The key to the visual display of information includes choosing the appropriate chart to support the text. For example, if the objective is to convey trends, the time series chart may be suitable. It does not, however, display the relative ratio of variables to each other as well as does the stacked bar chart. Those preparing the report will have to decide which of the two charts to use. But more important than use or output data is to identify how the library impacts the lives of the library's customers (outcome measures).

Why Do We Communicate?

Managers communicate the value of library in order to influence various stakeholders about the need and importance of the library in the lives of the individuals who use the library. If stakeholders understand the value of the library, they should be in a better position to balance various competing interests for financial and other resources when budgeting decisions are made.

The factors that influence credibility are expertise and trustworthiness. A library director who is active on campus or in the community will build trust and will be better received when making presentations about the library and its value. When presenting information about the use of a particular set of performance metrics it is important for this person to

- Ensure that the results of any survey that has been conducted are accurate and that the survey did not have any methodology problems (e.g., concerns about sample size and sample bias). Clearly indicate the reliability of the data as well as any shortcoming.
- Document the process for how the data for each metric were collected.
- Compare the results with the results of other comparable libraries.
- Contrast the results with those that are noted in the literature.

When Do We Communicate?

The process of communicating the value of the library is something that should occur throughout the year rather than simply releasing the library's written annual report. A combination of written and oral messages should be conveyed using press releases and formal and informal presentations before interested groups and the funding stakeholders.

The library can produce a range of written materials to communicate more effectively the message that it provides real value to the community. Among the other written materials that can be prepared are:

- Look for creative ways to use a human-interest perspective to make the contributions of the public library come alive in newspaper articles.
- Prepare an executive summary of each written report (no more than two pages).
- Every presentation should be well designed and have real visual appeal (consider using colorful graphics, charts, and so forth).
- Use the library's monthly newsletter to focus on the progress being made to achieve the goals of the library.
- Prepare an article to submit to one of the professional library journals documenting your experiences and results.
- Perhaps more important, think about preparing an article discussing your experiences for the higher education administrator's perspective or the municipal professional management association.

The library can prepare formal presentations (using PowerPoint slides and handouts) as well as be prepared to give informal, brief talks to small-group meetings. The hallmark of a good salesperson is to prepare a succinct "elevator speech," which summarizes the message. The library director and management team members, who are the "salespersons" for the library, should practice their elevator speech about the value of the library.

Storytelling puts information in context and is a way to make facts and figures come alive. Stories are how people make sense of things. Library managers should consistently collect and use "war stories." A good story is often the best way to convey the message about the value of the library and its information services. Stories have a human voice and help to communicate in a way that the listener will remember the message better. Begin your next presentation by saying, "Let me tell you a story . . ."

ASK FOR FEEDBACK

Ask a variety of stakeholders for a review and critique of the library's communication strategy and your particular presentation skills. Different people have different ways in which they prefer to receive and absorb information: visual, through a conversation, listening to a formal presentation, reading a brief synopsis, and so forth. Taking to heart the candid comments of stakeholders will allow you the opportunity to improve your presentation skills and fine-tune the message regarding the value of the public library so that it will resonate with local stakeholders.

Whatever measures are chosen, it is important to show trends over time just as corporations do in their annual reports. Showing data for the last five years will typically provide enough time and data to demonstrate any trends.

Concluding Thoughts

As the library director and members of the library's management team communicate with stakeholders, staff members, and customers, they should remember that

- Politics is at least as important as measuring library outcomes.
- Cultivate the library's stakeholders, even when you do not need anything.
- Do not oversell library services—over-deliver.[5] Look for ways to personalize services experienced by customers, whether in person or online.[6]
- Convey the message of the value of the library vividly but succinctly. Convert the library's annual budget to a cost per day per capita. Identity the number of days it takes for the entire population of the community to visit the library (total population divided by daily gate count times "x" number of days).

- Talk to library stakeholders one-on-one whenever possible.
- Put information into a context. Rather than using dry statistics, provide some context that will be understandable in the environment within which the library operates. For example, convert the annual number of people visiting the library (in person and online) to the number of times a nearby football stadium would be filled up.
- Present information in terms that the audience will understand. Translate numbers, be they dollars or statistics, into terms that have a real associative meaning so that the bottom line message of the library will be heard, understood, and remembered.
- Communicating the value of the library is "Job # 1" for the library director. Make sure to devote the time and energy to always be prepared to deliver the library's message.

Exercises

1. How might library management communicate evaluation study results to library staff, Friends' groups, prospective donors, boards of trustees, institutional stakeholders, state legislators, and library users?

2. You want to display graphically the relative ratio of expenses for collections ($990,315), personnel ($2,103,775), and other operating expenditures ($531,509). What type of visual would you consider using?

(Answers to these questions are in the "Appendix" at the back of the book. We encourage different members of a library staff to work on the exercises together and to discuss the results.)

NOTES

1. Gary M. Klass, *Just Plain Data Analysis: Finding, Presenting, and Interpreting Social Science Data* (Lanham, MD: Rowman & Littlefield, 2008), 33–35, 45.

2. Richard Saul Wurman, *Information Anxiety 2* (Indianapolis, IN: Que, 2001).

3. Peter Hernon, Robert E. Dugan, and Danuta Nitecki, *Engaging in Evaluation and Assessment Research* (Santa Barbara, CA: Libraries Unlimited, 2011), 179–99.

4. Minnesota State Colleges & Universities, "Accountability Dashboard," www.mnscu.edu/board/accountability/index.html.

5. Tom Peters, *Thriving on Chaos* (New York: Pan Books, 1989).

6. Kevin Davis, "The Changing Role of the Business Librarian," *Knowledge Management* (December 1998), http://enterprise.supersites.net/knmagn2/km199812/fc1.htm.

11

POSITIVE
ORGANIZATIONAL
CHANGE

istorically in libraries evaluation focused on collections, their development and management, and an array of input metrics to demonstrate in today's language simple cost distribution (budget allocation) and effectiveness. Evaluation as a social science activity in library and information science (LIS), however, emerged in the 1970s with a focus on planning and performance metrics. That emphasis has continued to broaden from how the library sees itself to include the role it plays in the lives of customers, the institution or broader organization, and other stakeholders.

Evaluation might examine particular programs or services, or even the entire organization. As Kim Cameron writes, at one time the concept of organizational effectiveness was the key to understanding organizational success. In his review of the foundations of organizational effectiveness, he highlights five models or perspectives:

1. the goal model, which centers on the accomplishment of goals and objectives;

2. the resource-dependent model, which focuses on the acquisition of needed resources;
3. the internal congruence model, which looks at the extent to which organizations function internally in a consistent and efficient way;
4. the strategic (or multiple) constituencies model, which deals with the satisfaction of dominant stakeholders and strategic constituencies; and
5. the human relations model, which centers on a collaborative climate and the ability to engage the workforce.

Among the five the first has been the most prevalent in the LIS literature; however, the fourth model received some attention in the 1980s and 1990s.

Outside LIS, the five models were integrated into the Competing Values Framework, which clusters them into four quadrants that demonstrate their flexibility or stability, and internal maintenance or external positioning. Further, "organizational effectiveness is significantly higher when activities related to innovation and creativity are associated with all four quadrants as part of an improvement strategy."[1] Neither the framework nor the five models have gained universal acceptance given the complexity of effectiveness evaluation, which involves more than one indicator or perspective. Still, as Cameron concludes, "it must be emphasized that it is only the concept of organizational effectiveness that faded, not the need to assess organizational performance, make judgments about excellence, or enhance organizational performance. Effectiveness as a phenomenon, in other words, was not abandoned; rather, researchers replaced it with other concepts."[2]

Cameron points out that positive organizational scholarship (POS) is a substitute for effectiveness, because it draws on the full spectrum of organizational theories and is not limited to a single definition of effectiveness. This concept focuses on outcomes, processes, employee resilience, capacity-building, and developing the workforce. In so doing it might be connected with change management and organizations in the process of accomplishing a vision of the future, one that reflects dramatic change from the present.

To make POS more acceptable to LIS, the umbrella concept might be renamed positive organizational change (POC); regardless, the end result is recognized as theoretically informed applications, supported by data. The goal is to cultivate extraordinary individual and organizational performance, while ensuring healing and restoration, where necessary, among members of organizational leadership and staff. This goal really embraces leadership theories such as servant leadership and resonant leadership, and thereby connects change to the concept of leadership. After all, the focus is on what is positive in organizations and the people who guide and change them.

Institutional Effectiveness

Despite the movement away from organizational effectiveness, there is an effort at the state level to recast organizational effectiveness as institutional effectiveness applicable to higher education. The Lumina Foundation, for instance, connects effectiveness with productivity and defines productivity as a simple ratio: educational resources used over the number of degrees produced. According to Social Program Evaluators and Consultants, Inc., which produced a consulting report for the foundation, productivity "is a measure of how well inputs are utilized to produce [an] output. It combines the concepts of effectiveness, efficiency and quality."[3] This definition therefore avoids any need to consider student learning outcomes or to focus on learning at all. Only metrics that track graduation rate become important, and institutional planning should focus on meeting or excelling on this one student outcome. Further, institutional productivity focuses on graduation rate and student learning is assumed. The assumption is that if students graduate and join the workforce in the state, they learned. The goal from a state perspective is to benefit the local economy with an educated workforce.[4] Clearly, library managers need to monitor developments inside and outside the institution or broader organization and new metrics that emerge. They might take a leadership role in assessing different metrics and settling on those most important to the parent body and the library.

Planning

As discussed in chapter 1, evaluation occurs within the context of planning; the purpose of evaluation is to generate data that can be judged in some context and used to make improvements in programs and services and to demonstrate the value of the library to the broader organization or institution, the community served, and strategic stakeholders. Part of accountability focuses on the appropriate distribution and expenditure of the budget and ensuring that the collections, programs, services, and the physical facilities have the intended results or impact. Evaluation, therefore, plays a role in documenting performance or operational accountability while enabling the library to contribute further to the well-being of the community.

Creating Positive Organizational Change

This section of the chapter offers encouragement for librarians and library school students as they experiment with the types of evaluation activities discussed in this book.[5] Those activities are essential for complying with demands for accountability, selecting relevant metrics, tracking customer satisfaction, monitoring the return on investment, and addressing the other issues covered in this book. Increasingly customers are placed at the center of evaluation, and metrics reflect market penetration, how libraries respond to changing use patterns and expectations in a competitive marketplace, cost benefit, and a desire to improve the customer experience.

In the academic environment, James G. Neal, university librarian at Columbia University, suggested that ROI is a "miscalculated, defensive and risky strategy."[6] However, some stakeholders expect to have data about ROI and they want the data to be as accurate as possible. With this in mind, we were cognizant of Neal's criticisms as we developed chapters 8 and 9. Such criticism is not a substitute for inaction, but serves as a reminder that librarians must rely on reliable and valid data and, in footnotes, explain any shortcomings.

The following ten tidbits are organized around ideas that can be quickly scanned and understood. Those that seem irrelevant may be skipped, while those that are interesting may be further explored elsewhere in this book and beyond. In short, the tidbits may be read either as a summary or an introduction to your journey into the evaluation of an academic or public library and how its infrastructure serves the community.

TIDBIT ONE
ACCOUNTABILITY IS PART OF LIBRARIANSHIP

A common refrain is that "I did not go to library school to engage in number crunching. I really want to help people locate the information and resources they need." As library school graduates soon recognize, advancement in the profession is often to managerial positions, and managers need evidence for setting and monitoring budgets, and engaging in decision making and planning. Management involves more than making assumptions and hoping that others are persuaded by conjecture. Strategic stakeholders want to know about trends, how the library responds to a changing fiscal climate, and how the library manages its resources to meet strategic priorities. Accountability, which is here to stay, requires libraries and other organizations to have persuasive numbers to justify actions and expenditures.

TIDBIT TWO
AUSTERITY INCREASES THE NEED FOR EVALUATION

Ironically, the opposite is true: austerity leads to demands for greater accountability and should result in more evaluations. There is need to gather a wider set of metrics (see chapters 4 and 5) than previously and to do so on a continuous basis. Strategic stakeholders and library managers want to know what is occurring—how well the mission is being met, and, for academic libraries, compliance with accreditation standards. Libraries need to focus on priorities and having the evidence to demonstrate progress in meeting those priorities. As appropriate, the evidence can be used to make course corrections and, for many libraries, regrettably to demonstrate how they are doing more with fewer resources.

TIDBIT THREE
LIBRARIANS ARE ENGAGED IN ORGANIZATIONAL CHANGE MANAGEMENT

Change is part of every organization that intends to survive and thrive. Resistance to change may create a disruptive work environment in which workers may be less focused on fulfilling their daily roles and activities.

This leads to a reduced level of efficiency and output. To avoid such situations and keep the library focused on its mission and vision at a time of rapid change, library managers need to know where the organization is headed and to manage change. Much of the change may be evolutionary and incremental but it might also be radical—moving the library in completely new directions and abandoning certain routines and functions. As highlighted in chapter 1, Rush Miller maintains that this "is not a time for retrenchment and timidity but for expansion and boldness . . . Even in a recession, we should seize the opportunities it affords us to question our traditions in light of the needs of our users in the digital age. In fact, I say, Damn the Recession, Full Speed Ahead!"[7]

TIDBIT FOUR

EVALUATION IS NOT BRAIN SURGERY

There are two types of evaluation activities: (1) those that require the application of research as an inquiry process, and (2) the types of activities discussed in this book. The first type requires a knowledge of social science research and a special skill set, especially with the conduct of quantitative research. The type of activities discussed in this book requires high-quality data sets that are regularly updated and inserted in a management information system. When libraries focus on input, process, and output metrics, they should apply standard procedures for data collection and strive for data that are reliable and valid. Clearly, this is good management and not brain surgery.

TIDBIT FIVE

**MEANINGFUL EVALUATION FOCUSES
ON CUSTOMERS AND DEMONSTRATING
THE VALUE OF THE LIBRARY TO THEM**

This tidbit serves as a reminder that libraries are not warehouses of books and other resources that are rarely used. Academic and public libraries serve their communities and rely on their support. Customers and customer service, therefore, are critical for them to address, with the goal of being customer-centric organizations. For this reason, customer expectations are important to know and meet (or exceed). In terms of the customer service literature the goal is to delight customers and make them enthusiastic supporters of the organization. Customers should realize that use of the library is a cost-effective proposition: they can receive more value than what they expended financially.

TIDBIT SIX

THE HARDEST THING IS TO START . . . "JUST DO IT"

Evaluation may seem overwhelming and librarians may ask, "Where do we start?" The answer is to start from a set of strategic directions and the strategic plan. If these do not exist develop them.[8] Once they exist, we suggest chapters 4 and 5 offer a good beginning. Select a key set of metrics, develop and put in place a set of procedures for their collection, and create a management information system. Note that Counting Opinions offers such a system, one with access to data sets from IMLS and ACRL. Having access to such a system saves some steps, but the library still needs to engage in regular data collection and, over time, expand the set of metrics collected and used. As libraries do so they should not forget chapters 6 and 7, focusing on satisfaction and service quality. In today's environment, greater attention is given to satisfaction, and the library may be only one unit of the institution or broader organization being evaluated and compared—valuing what customers say and think.

TIDBIT SEVEN

PLAY WITH THE VARIOUS CONCEPTS

We cannot stress this tidbit enough. We encourage readers to review the chapter exercises, perhaps in groups, and to generate discussion about what is most meaningful to "their" library. The library director and other managers should lead this discussion, with stakeholders attending at some point. At the same time, they can develop additional exercises, ones tailored to the needs of the particular learning organization, practice data collection, and relate data collection to the planning process.

TIDBIT EIGHT

MAKE EVALUATION PART OF YOUR REGULAR WORK

This tidbit follows from the previous one. The goal of those discussions is not to engage in an academic exercise; rather, which activities can be best used for strategic advantage and demonstrating accountability? Part of the discussion is about incorporating data collection into the regular work activities of every unit in the library. Following that discussion it is important to see that such incorporation is actually done and the desired results emerge and change occurs.

TIDBIT NINE
SHARE THE RESULTS
Sharing involves extending the discussion of metrics beyond chapter 4 and embracing chapter 5. This may require discussions with stakeholders, including city, state, and other auditors, or at least awareness of their expectations. Sharing involves getting feedback on what you are doing, the data sets used, and future plans.

TIDBIT TEN
HAVE A MANAGEMENT INFORMATION SYSTEM
This tidbit relates to some previously mentioned tidbits, but is essential for ongoing planning, decision making, and accountability. A few libraries maintain a balanced scorecard for their system,[9] but most libraries do not. For this reason, we recommend a system such as the one offered by Counting Opinions. Whatever system is used, its purpose is to ensure that it contains the types of metrics highlighted in chapters 4 and 5 that are most important to that organization. As needed, managers can readily produce data reflecting the return on investment and other factors relevant to key stakeholders.

SUMMARY
Perhaps a theme cutting across various tidbits is that library managers should not let any evidence gathered remain unused. If they collect evidence, it should be for a purpose—one that improves service and advances accountability. Evaluation does not occur in a vacuum; it advances change management and is a critical part of a learning organization.

Concluding Thoughts

Evaluation, a multifaceted component of planning and management, applies to all facets of a library's infrastructure (collections and services, facilities, technology use, and staff) as the library responds to many challenges and shapes change. What it means to be an academic or public library in the twenty-first century is evolving due, for instance, to constantly developing and changing digital technologies, changing publishing models, new sources of funding, a more diverse community served, a shift in libraries from serving as a place where people consume information to a setting in which people learn from each other and interact socially.[10] Complicating matters, many librarians still do not like the fact that libraries are not exempt from the application of businesslike practices such as ROI. Central to any academic or public library today is meeting the expectations of customers and stakeholders, while managing change. All of these activities require the types of data discussed in this book and a focus on knowing, that is, knowing about shifting use patterns, benchmarking services to peer organizations, trends in accountability and service performance, insights gained from the use of ROI and the community's reaction to such data characterization, market penetration, and so on. Evaluation involves monitoring, understanding, documenting, and improving—all of which is essential for librarians who serve as managers and shape the organizational response to change. Part of change is ensuring that the staff have the necessary skills and competencies to meet the vision set for a twenty-first-century library. Evaluation, therefore, focuses on the present but shapes the near future.

Exercises

1. The University of West Florida libraries calculated its institutional return on investment on the following services provided during a fiscal year:

   Students studying in the library (average annual cost per hour to open = *XXX*; factor in 10 percent of gate count stayed one hour; students using a day study carrel: day carrels are loaned for 6 hours/per use);

   Borrowing books, e-books, DVDs, and laptops (assumption: the book is used; used books are 20 percent of the average cost of a new book *YYY*; average Kindle e-book is *ZZZ*; they used 20 percent of that cost even though the e-books are academic-based and thereby costlier; average cost for each DVD if rented; hardware and installed software);

Students or faculty members asking reference questions or meeting with reference librarians for individual research consultations (values assigned for reference questions range from $5.00 [Regent University] to $43 [Suffolk University]; individual research consultations with reference staff; Georgia Tech and Cornell charge $75/hour for library research services);

Conducting library instruction sessions (number of library instruction sessions; use the cost of a research consultation; average library instruction session = 1 hour); and

Students or faculty members using subscription data bases when off campus (estimate that 5 percent of occurrences saved the student or faculty member from driving 30 miles round trip to the library; saved 1 gallon of gas).

Calculations (using an Excel spreadsheet) are based on the number of occurrences (service outputs) multiplied by an informal and conservative market value of the occurrence to calculate a summed value for the services. The summed value is divided by the sum of the libraries' personnel and operating expenditures. As a result, it is determined that, for every dollar expended, at least $*MMM* is returned for the services identified (see http://lgdata.s3-website-us-east-1.amazonaws.com/docs/1663/315728/pace-roi-fy2011.pdf for FY 2011).

For a public or other academic library, would you substitute or add services? Which ones? Why? Would you change any of the values assigned? Next, construct an institutional ROI that would be meaningful to report to upper administration.

2. Using table 6.1, construct a staff satisfaction survey that produces a gap so that you can calculate both a net promoter score and an opportunity index. Once the instrument is drafted, pretest it on some colleagues and run a trial survey with some student workers. As you construct the instrument,

how might the questions relate to planning and customer service?

3. Which would be more meaningful to your library, a study of customer satisfaction or service quality? Discuss.

4. Develop ROI but one applicable to reference service. What variables would you include? What would be the data sources? Discuss.

5. Develop ROI for another service area. What variables would you include? What would be the data sources? Discuss.

(Answers to these questions are in the "Appendix" at the back of the book. We encourage different members of a library staff to work on the exercises together and to discuss the results.)

NOTES

1. Kim Cameron, "Organizational Effectiveness: Its Demise and Re-Emergence through Positive Organizational Scholarship," in *Great Minds in Management: The Process of Theory Development*, ed. Michael A. Hitt and Ken G. Smith (London: Oxford University Press, 2005), 309. See also www.bus.umich.edu/Positive/PDF/Cameron-OE%20and%20POS.pdf (p. 5).

2. Ibid., 316; page 12 on PDF.

3. Social Program Evaluators and Consultants, Inc., *Year One Evaluation of Lumina Foundation's Higher Education Productivity Work in Seven States* (Detroit, MI: Social Program Evaluators and Consultants, Inc., 2011), 1–2, www.specassociates.org/docs/Year%20One%20Evaluation%20of%20 Lumina%20Foundation's%20HE%20Productivity%20Work%20in%20 Seven%20States.pdf. See also National Governors Association, Center for Best Practices, *Complete to Compete: From Information to Action: Revamping Higher Education Accountability Systems* (2011), www.nga.org/files/live/ sites/NGA/files/pdf/1107C2CACTIONGUIDE.PDF.

4. Peter Hernon, Robert E. Dugan, and Candy Schwartz, *Higher Education Outcomes Assessment for the Twenty-First Century* (Santa Barbara, CA: Libraries Unlimited, 2013).

5. This section draws on Peter Hernon, Robert E. Dugan, and Danuta A. Nitecki, *Engaging in Evaluation and Assessment Research* (Santa Barbara, CA: Libraries Unlimited, 2011), 211–20.

6. James G. Neal, "Stop the Madness: The Insanity of ROI and the Need for New Qualitative Measures of Academic Library Success," ACRL Confer-

ence (2011), 424, www.ala.org/acrl/sites/ala.org.acrl/files/content/conferences/confsandpreconfs/national/2011/papers/stop_the_madness.pdf.

7. Rush Miller, "Damn the Recession, Full Speed Ahead," *Journal of Library Administration* 52, no. 1 (2012): 3, 17.

8. See Joseph R. Matthews, *Strategic Planning and Management for Library Managers* (Westport, CT: Libraries Unlimited, 2005).

9. See Joseph R. Matthews, *Scorecards for Results: A Guide for Developing a Library Balanced Scorecard* (Westport, CT: Libraries Unlimited, 2008).

10. For an excellent discussion of trends, see Ken Roberts, *Facing the Future: A Vision Document for British Columbia's Public Libraries*, http://commons.bclibraries.ca/wp-content/uploads/2012/12/Facing-the-Future-A-Report-on-the-future-of-libraries-for-the-Province-of-British-Columbia.pdf.

APPENDIX

Answers to Chapter Exercises

CHAPTER ONE

1. Evaluation should first focus on whether the library maintains records on the number of questions asked and answered at the reference desk, for what time period, and how good (reliable and valid) those statistics are. Depending on the quality of the data, the library might engage in data collection and compare what it finds to what other comparable libraries have found. Part of the data collection might focus on other means by which customers ask questions—virtually and other.

2. However, before engaging in data collection, the staff should review the existing literature on the topic from search engines such as Google and library-related literature. For example, see Gabriela Sonntag and Felicia Palsson, "No Longer the Sacred Cow—No Longer a Desk: Transforming Reference Service to Meet 21st Century User Needs," *Library Philosophy and Practice* (2007), www.webpages .uidaho.edu/~mbolin/sonntag-palsson.htm.

3. Develop a typology of the different ways in which customers might pose questions such as in person, by telephone, by e-mail, through a social network, and so on. A companion typology divides questions in ready reference and other forms commonly found in the literature of library reference service. Through data collection, the question can be answered (but only for the time period for what data were collected, assuming the investigation did not involve the use of probability sampling to project the findings to a time period such as a month or year).

4. This answer is covered in the previous question.

5. This question returns to the literature and examining search engines and library-related literature. There might also be conference presentations on the topic, and staff might know of instances of libraries pursuing other models. As the staff search the literature they should not forget to check for scenarios that offer different depictions of the future; see, for instance, Action-Based Research, "Scenario 5: What's Happening at the Reference Desk," http://alaworkshopdata.wordpress.com/datasets/scenario-5-whats-happening-at-the-reference-desk/.

6. The answer is covered in the previous question.

7. Ultimately a public library might decide to retain reference desk service, but what changes are introduced, depending on the findings?

CHAPTER TWO

1. SPICE-structured research question:

   S (setting): What is the context of the question? Reference desk in a library.

   P (perspective): Who are the users/potential users of the outcomes? Those asking reference questions.

   I (intervention): What will staff have to do? Change in the skills and knowledge of those staffing the reference desk.

   C (comparison): What are alternatives? Staffing the reference desk with paraprofessionals or professionals.

E (evaluation): How might we measure whether the intervention is successful? Measure the changes in reference transactions as recorded and analyzed; or measure and analyze customer satisfaction.

Research question: Is there a change (increase or decrease, type of question asked) in reference transactions when staffing the reference desk with paraprofessionals instead of professional librarians?

Research question: Is there a change in user satisfaction with their interactions with the reference desk when staffed by paraprofessionals instead of professional librarians?

2. Reference/Inquiries

3. Library and information science databases (e.g., Library Literature; Library, Information Science & Technology Abstracts [LISTA] is available free to any library currently subscribing to any EBSCO-host database). See also Peter Hernon, Robert E. Dugan, and Danuta A. Nitecki, *Engaging in Evaluation and Assessment Research* (Libraries Unlimited, 2011, 23–24); library and information science journals, including journals available through Association of College and Research Libraries and the Public Library Association; web resources which may be found in institutional repositories or in other grey literature; and write-ups of library conference panels and other presentations. Additionally, literature might be identified through searches in web search engines such as Google Scholar, and then retrieved through interlibrary loan.

4. Case studies: someone may have already addressed this research question; comparative studies: studies comparing differences of paraprofessionals and professional staffing public desks; descriptive surveys: a survey(s) may have already asked users about the differences between paraprofessionals and professional staffing public desks; focus group interviews with customers about their perspectives of differing service quality; gap analyses: write-ups of service quality expectations versus satisfaction; program evaluations which have evaluated staffed reference desks; and randomized controlled trials: a library may have conducted this research using control groups.

5. There might be local data, including customer feedback: your library may already have some feedback that can be aligned with this research question; library personnel observations: and your library may already have compiled some observations that can be aligned with this research question; usage data: again, data may already exist that may align with this question. Another source would be discussion with colleagues. For example, another member of your regional consortium may have already studied this question.

6. First would be validity. Is there discernible bias in the write-up? There could be if the study reported that the result was that paraprofessionals are a disaster when staffing the reference desk if the article was written by a professional. Is the study reliable? Is the research instrument available, and can the study conducted be replicated in your library with manageable adjustments reflecting the local context? One may also utilize a checklist to guide the reviewer through research articles in a systematic way that may also be applicable and useful.

7. Apply the evidence to the decision-making process and make a meaningful decision. Rely on your formal and informal learning, practitioner experience and tacit knowledge, and reflective knowledge.

8. All three. Structure relates to the physical assets that enable a service to be provided and how they are configured, in this case, staffing the reference desk. Process relates to how things are done within a service. Is there a difference in the paraprofessional's or the professional's process when responding to questions from customers? An outcome is the effect that a service has on its users. Is there a measurable difference to the user of who answers their questions?

9. Collect the types of questions asked by users based upon the staffing of the reference desk and the time, by analysis of transactions via transactional logging such as the contact source of the question, such as face-to-face or virtual; the number of directional questions; the number of questions seeking technology help or other assistance with non-information resources; the number of questions

that would require the knowledge and use of available resources to answer; customer type (e.g., student, senior citizen, and gender); the length of time spent by reference desk personnel with each customer.

Collect user perceptions of reference assistance received after the assistance has been provided by user surveys and focus group interviews.

10. Direct stakeholders: library staff because they will have a direct interest in a study concerning staffing public service desks; and customers of the reference desk because a change in staffing may influence whether or not they continue to use the reference desk for assistance.

Indirect stakeholders: senior institutional managers because it directly affects constituents and it may have an influence on the costs to staff the reference desk; and other librarians who may have the same question concerning staffing the reference desk.

Reporting could come in a variety of means, such as blogs, wikis, and personal or professional websites; presenting a paper at a conference; taking part in a poster session at a national, regional, or state conference; conducting a workshop, session or webinar; participating in face-to-face or virtual discussion groups; and using communications systems such as discussion lists, e-mail, and social networking tools to increase awareness of the work undertaken.

CHAPTER THREE

The three questions are ones for discussion as there is no single or simple answer that applies to all libraries. Individual libraries might even take peer or competitive organizations into account when answering the questions.

In developing their answers, they might even examine the ACRLMetrics or the IMLS equivalent data set and the assorted variables included.

CHAPTER FOUR

1. Inputs, processes, and outputs.

2. Inputs involve the infrastructure common to all types of libraries: collections, staff, technologies, and facilities. Inputs are often measured by attributes, such as their quantity or budget.

3. Processes, also known as throughputs, convert inputs into outputs. They are most often captured in terms of efficiencies, such as workload indicators. For example, it takes a staff person (which is an input) thirty minutes to catalog a monograph, or books are reshelved within six hours of their return.

4. Outputs are often measured in terms of cost, quality, timeliness, availability, and accessibility. The number of items circulated during a twelve-month period is an output measure. Other examples of output measures include the costs to answer a reference question (another output is the number of reference questions answered) and the number of interlibrary loan transactions.

5. Quantitative mechanisms are usually discrete numbers found through simple counting, analyzing transaction logs, budget and expenditure analysis, discovering direct and indirect costs (e.g., cost of mediated interlibrary loan/document delivery), and longitudinal trend analysis. Qualitative mechanisms are more subjective; data are found through performance evaluation, interviews, surveys, the use of consultants or external review teams, unobtrusive studies, process analysis, job factor analysis, organizational structure analysis, and specific expenditure analysis (e.g., by discipline [genre] and format, and their relationship to expressed need).

6. A starting place would be to follow up with the user (if possible) to learn the nature of the complaint, such as learning from the user that there is not enough comfortable seating at which to read the daily print newspaper. Quantify the mixture of seating available in user spaces. For example, what is the ratio of seats at equipment to non-equipment? How many seats are located at tables versus as individual seats? What is the ratio of lounge seats to all individual seats? Looking at these ratios may reveal that a high percentage of seats are at equipment or tables, and that individual seats are mostly limited to beanbag chairs in the children's area, while the user is seeking comfortable, individual seating at which to read the print newspaper.

7. The book may be shelved out of place. However, an evaluative study may learn about the turnaround time concerning the return of a loaned book to its being reshelved. A time and motion study of reshelving books may reveal an interesting internal issue, such as that it takes, on average, three days to shelve a returned book. The local library managers may consider this as too long a time period and the process of reshelving books needs to be addressed. How? Maybe there are too few staff reshelving books. The study may also find that books are reshelved on Mondays and Thursdays because, as staff tell you, that is when most books are returned. Furthermore, the evaluative study may find that staff reshelve returned books for just two hours rather than until the return carts are emptied, leaving unshelved books on the return carts when the two hours set aside for reshelving are reached. Therefore, a book returned on Wednesday would be checked in (identified as available by the automated system) but, because it was not reshelved on Thursday because the time for reshelving was reached before the book was reshelved, will not be reshelved until the following Monday at the earliest. Library managers may use this data to make an informed decision about the process of reshelving books.

8. A couple of output measures may help. The first would be to determine a program's start and end time frame. Also, find out how many people attended the program. Hopefully the library gathers and compiles entrance gate counts. How many people entered the library in the hour before the program began? Compare that count to the gate counts for the same time and day of week when there is no program activity. This analysis will help one learn about the program's draw. It may also help the library's managers to realize that not everyone who entered the library attends the program but may facilitate another's attendance. For example, a parent brings a child into the library for a program, but does not attend the program herself. From a service point of view, you may want to consider additional services for those not attending the program; for example, the library may consider offering coffee in a designated area for the parents of the children attending the program. The library may also discover that this designated area becomes a place where the parents converse with each other.

Another output to review is circulation statistics during the periods before, during, and after the program. Are there quantifiable changes in typical circulation transactions during that period? It may be that those attending a program then borrow materials from the library, a type of "one-stop shopping trip"—attend a program and borrow books and media. If possible, quantify what materials were checked out during the periods in the evaluative study to learn if any were related to the program by genre and/or topic. For example, if the program was a poetry reading, was there a measureable increase in the number of poetry books checked out following the program?

9. An output. Satisfaction is the expression of customer-expressed importance and relevance of what they received from the library in relation to what they expected or needed and wanted. Outcomes, also known as impacts, are the result that the library's service has on an individual's quality of life, and the library's measured or perceived contribution to the value of its services.

10. This evaluative study would involve inputs, processes, and outputs. First, are there long lines all day every day, or is it more sporadic? Library management would want to ask library users about when the queues occur and also observe the lines themselves. If sporadic, then discover the times when the lines form, and for how long there are lines before they dissipate. The times during the day, and the days of the week are identified. Then, knowing about several inputs and outputs would be useful.

First, how many staff are at the circulation desk when the lines occur? Why is this important? It may be, of course, that the desk is understaffed to meet these peak times. You may decide to increase staffing at the desk. However, this may not be feasible from a cost point of view. An alternative to consider would have designated library staff on call, summoned to the circulation desk from their usual activity when circulation desk personnel perceive the need. How may one perceive need? You may want to borrow a practice from retail. For example, if there are five people queued, call for additional help.

Second, it may be the classification of staff at the desk that is causing the queue. Desk personnel with little experience may be slowing the line as they learn to function. As a result team them up with experienced personnel until the circulation transaction becomes routine. Library managers may also decide not to train new desk personnel during peak transactions times.

Third, it may be the activities occurring behind the desk that are causing the queue. Observe the activities. How long does each transaction, by type of transaction, take? It may take longer for a person to check out equipment than books or media. Usage policy forms may need to be signed, and the desk staff may make a last check of the equipment before handing it to the user. Additionally, more equipment may be transacting than books and media. If that is the case, the library managers may want to establish a "book and media express lane" at the circulation desk during such peak times. Or, add another desk person to the equipment loan function.

Fourth, it takes longer to check out twenty books than ten books. Observation may inform library managers that queues form when the majority of users are borrowing more than fifteen books at a time. That information is useful to collect in order to communicate this behavior as a reason for the queues to users.

The solutions offered and implemented should themselves be evaluated to learn if they solved the queue problem. One indication that the problem has been resolved is that complaints have decreased, and users may even comment that the lines are faster than before. Satisfaction increases. Second, if the library is using personnel on call for circulation, then count the number of times per hour that the staff on call are summoned to the desk and how long they stay. If they are staying longer than you expected or hoped (a measurable objective for the planning and evaluation of this change in service), then assigning another person to the circulation desk may be in order. Another evaluation would determine if the queues disappeared when the most experienced personnel staff the desk. Another evaluative study would review the results of creating the express lane or adding a second person to loaning equipment.

11. Cost studies use inputs, processes, and outputs. In the case of reference questions, the inputs are the costs incurred such as staffing and supplies, the throughput is the time involved to answer the question, and the output is the number of answered questions.

Please note a couple of issues here. First, this is measuring the cost of questions answered, which is very different than determining the unit cost for questions asked. For this study, we are looking at the reference question as an output, not as an input. Second, costs to answer a question will not identify the quality of the answer. It could be the wrong answer to the reference question.

To make the simplest calculation:

- determine the number of hours each person working at the reference desk is there for the period of time being evaluated. A full twelve months, aligned with the library's fiscal year, would be ideal. Include the hours spent off-desk answering reference questions generated by users at the desk, over the phone, via e-mail, and so on, again by the person.

- determine the hourly cost for each person who worked at the reference desk. Then, multiply that cost per hour by the number of hours each person reported as working at the desk for a cost per person for the time period being evaluated.

- if possible, calculate the fringe benefits (if paid as part of the library's operating budget) per person for the time spent at the reference desk (this would be a percentage of their total fringe benefit costs for the time spent on the reference desk function).

- sum the cost for all of the personnel who worked on the reference desk function, including fringe benefits if possible.

- include, as possible, other direct operating costs related to answering reference questions, such as the cost of the desk's telephone and supplies.

- sum the personnel costs with the other direct costs to arrive at a total cost; and

- divide this total cost by the number of questions answered. This yields a cost per question answered.

Although the cost per reference question answered is not the full cost because indirect costs are not included in the total cost, it is still a useful measure and one that can be studied annually and graphed on a time series chart to display a trend.

A more complicated calculation would include the granularity of the questions answered if the information was captured. For example, the library may be able to derive a cost per question as answered by professional staff versus support staff. The library may also want to determine the cost of questions answered face-to-face versus the telephone. Another would break out the costs by the time it took to answer the reference question, such as the cost for those taking less than ten minutes and those taking longer than ten minutes. Another factor would be user demographics—"who is receiving the answer"—if it is possible to learn about them.

The information from this evaluative study may result in the library examining reference desk staffing, discovering the busiest times of the day, week, month, and year, and the differences in costs depending upon the classification of the personnel answering the question or the communications source of the question. An objective may be to find the most cost effective manner for staffing the reference desk, with the lowest cost per question answered as the desired end.

12. Refer to the list in box 4.6. Here are selected metrics (generalized for academic, public, and special libraries) frequently used by one of the authors:

- circulation transactions per student/person in the area service population/employee

- reference transactions per student/person in the area service population/employee

- ILL loaned per student/person in the area service population/employee

- ILL borrowed per student/person in the area service population/employee

- ratio of interlibrary loan items loaned to items borrowed

- volumes held per student/person in the area service population/employee

- titles held per student/person in the area service population/employee

- serial subscriptions per student/person in the area service population/employee
- total expenditures per student/person in the area service population/employee
- total library materials resources expenditures per student/person in the area service population/employee
- monograph expenditures per student/person in the area service population/employee
- serials expenditures per student/person in the area service population/employee
- total electronic materials expenditures per student/person in the area service population/employee
- other library materials expenditures per student/person in the area service population/employee
- total staff expenditures per student/person in the area service population/employee
- salaries and wages expenditures for professional staff per student/person in the area service population/employee
- salaries and wages expenditures for support staff per student/person in the area service population/employee
- salaries and wages expenditures for student assistants per student/person in the area service population/employee
- percentage of total expenditures on collection materials and resources expenditures
- percentage of total expenditures on staff expenditures
- percentage of total expenditures on other operating expenditures
- professional staff in FTE
- support staff in FTE
- student assistants in FTE
- percentage professional staff to total staff
- percentage support staff to total staff
- percentage student assistants to total staff

CHAPTER FIVE

1. Libraries conduct external evaluations for several reasons:
   - the library wants to learn and demonstrate how its services impact users as individuals, support and contribute to the institution's mission by adding value, and benefit the general community it services. Results from external evaluations inform stakeholders about how well the library meets the needs and expectations of constituent groups and other stakeholders while aligning services and programs with the institution's mission and goals.
   - evaluative data, analysis, and results inform the library's short- and long-term planning as an input, as well as the library's immediate decision making.
   - the library wants to plan and implement changes by applying study findings to improve programs, services, management, and resources on behalf of customers, the institution, and the community.
   - studies may also identify and examine influential factors that are outside the library's managerial controls, such as inflation or the changing demographics of its service population.

2. If asked of ten librarians, there would be ten different responses. That is because it is important to evaluate services, programs, and resources from a local perspective, aligning the study areas with strategic initiatives that will be as different as libraries differ from each other. Additionally, it is important to consider external stakeholder information needs when planning and undertaking these evaluation studies.

3. **Collections.** Evaluating collections from an external stakeholder perspective will help to answer questions about the quality of the library's holdings as well as relevancy to its users. Also,
   - relevancy and currency of the holdings as expressed by the age of the collection, usually by call number
   - collection management such as weeding outdated materials from the collection, thereby improving quality
   - calculated conspectus factor

Personnel. Supporting library personnel costs usually consumes more than 50 percent of a library's annual budget allocation. Because of this ratio, external stakeholders want to be informed about the library's staff. And, for many libraries, staff are their most important infrastructure asset. Also,

- degrees held by the staff
- years of experience of library staff
- ratio of part-time to full-time staff
- recognitions and awards received by staff
- number of scholarly contributions, such as articles and books

Technologies. External stakeholders are interested in the technologies used by the library to provide and support services as well as ensuring that the library's need to continually refresh their deployment of technologies is worth the costs. Also,

- currency of equipment in use relative to the availability of equipment that can be used (e.g., the library may deploy desktop computers, but deploying ones running Windows 95 would not be considered current and therefore "old" and lacking quality)
- availability of resources 24/7 via networking technologies (e.g., access to full-text databases from home)
- alignment of technology available to need (e.g., who needs a mimeograph machine?)

Facilities. These are likely to be the library's most costly asset and their physical nature is also the most visible to external stakeholders. Additionally, external stakeholders are often asking about the costs to sustain the facility including deferred maintenance, renovations to keep its interior functional as use changes, and the costs for additions to increase the footprint as well as the costs to replace a no-longer usable structure. Also,

- sufficient number of seats available so that there is always an empty chair available
- every table is wired for network and electrical jacks
- the library's signage makes it easy for visitors to navigate

Services. External stakeholders are interested in the services provided and how well they meet, or do not meet, the needs of both users and nonusers. Also,

- library is open during hours when users are likely to use the library (e.g., the more hours open, the "better" the library as perceived by users)
- gate counts (the more physical visits, the busier the library; the busier the library, the "better" the library)
- accuracy of answers to reference questions
- provision of unique collections not generally available elsewhere by genre or need (e.g., locally focused special collections)
- usable meeting space for nonlibrary needs (may support publicly attended municipal meetings)
- provision of specific programs that one may not be able to find elsewhere (e.g., tax assistance, poetry readings, and art displays)

4. Many external stakeholders possess a financial perspective, and expressing value in terms of dollars may help to satisfy the stakeholders' financial questions. A simple calculation would be to multiply initial monograph circulation transactions by the average cost of a monograph. For example, if the library had 50,000 initial circulations and the average cost of a monograph assigned by the library was $10, the formula would be:

50,000 initial circulations times $10/book
= $500,000 worth of books circulated.

The library should use initial circulation rather than including renewals because a renewal only extends time available. If the book was returned, it may not circulate again during the time of the evaluation. Second, use a conservative figure when assigning a value for a circulated book. Consider a circulated monograph as "used," and a recommended practice is to price it at 20 percent of its list price. It is good practice to underestimate rather than overestimate value.

The library can also take it one step further. Determine the funding amount the library spent on monographs the last fiscal year. Let's say it was $100,000. An "elevator speech" return on investment may point out to an external stakeholder that for the $100,000 invested in books (the stakeholder may not understand the use of "monographs"), $500,000 worth of books circulated, there is a return on investment of $5.00 of services for every $1.00 invested in books.

5. Evaluating the savings from participating in programs that realize positive economies of scale demonstrates the library's financial efficiency, which is always appreciated and understood by external stakeholders with a mature financial perspective. Additionally, stakeholders will be interested in learning how the library leveraged those savings to increase and improve services to users. Libraries have been participating in economies of scale projects for decades; this example of cooperation is ingrained in most library cultures.

6. External pressures are worth evaluating so that they may be explained to external stakeholders who ask questions or have concerns about library services and costs that may be beyond the library's control or influence. Several pressures include:

   inflation—costs, sometimes predictable but often not, and therefore difficult to budget which are passed on by the multiplicity of library vendors who themselves are subjected to inflationary increases from their suppliers

   price of fuel—the library has no control over what is charged at the gas pump and the result may be that a library has to curtail or even shut down vehicle-based mobile services because of the price of fuel. Additionally, shipping costs increase as the price of fuel increases.

   weather—bad weather may adversely affect the number of days the library is open and thereby reduce gate counts, and initial circulation increases in area unemployment may result in reductions to the revenue available to support library operations.

7. External stakeholders with a business perspective are comfortable with calculations demonstrating return on investment. An important consideration is what services and costs the library includes in its calculation. It is also important for the library to underestimate rather than to overestimate unit costs (e.g., the value assigned to a book) in an effort to produce a conservative yet favorable return on investment for the interested stakeholders.

Usage
- gate counts
- asking a reference question
- using a research guide
- using a reference book
- using a newspaper or magazine
- database searches conducted
- downloads of full-text articles
- downloads of e-books
- using library resources online from a location outside of the physical library
- borrowing adult, young adult, and children's books
- borrowing audiobooks
- borrowing audiovisual media
- borrowing museum passes
- using interlibrary loan
- borrowing a laptop computer
- using a desktop computer connected to the Internet
- user accessibility to Wi-Fi service
- meeting room use
- attendance at adult, young adult, and children's programming

Assets
- the dollar value assigned to the collection
- the dollar value assigned to the physical facility

The assets in this category would be capital assets. Often these assets are assigned a value for property insurance purposes. For a library, the value should be the replacement value—what it would cost to replace the collection or facility if it should experience a total loss.

8. Library personnel salaries and wages. Salaries and wages are often the largest expenditure from the library's budget allocation. These salaries and wages are then reinvested by the staff into the geopolitical area as they pay rent, buy groceries, dine out, and so on. Although some libraries expend more than 50 percent of their budget allocation to develop and support collections in a multiplicity of formats, these expenditures usually have little impact on the locality because the information vendors are situated throughout the United States, and even the world. External stakeholders are often surprised by the library's local economic effect as demonstrated by the multiplier effect.

9. An evaluation study would identify the type of partnership: cooperation, coordination, or collaboration. The study could also evaluate the frequency of occurrences of the partnerships as well as a ratio of partnerships to non-partnerships (this question seeks to learn about the lack of partnerships), and the partnerships' impact on achieving student learning outcomes as planned.

   The evaluation study may expand its scope to identify weakness in the partnership's instruction and support services that could be improved in the ongoing effort to support learning and teaching effectively.

   The results from this study would be of interest to the school/college stakeholders interested in finding out what contributes to, as well as facilitates, a student's achievement of identified learning outcomes.

10. Stakeholders interested in the library are often interested in how the library "stacks up" with other libraries identified as peers. Comparisons help stakeholders understand the context in which library services and operations are provided and measured. Specifically,

- library visits per student/person in the area service population (also known as "capita")
- circulation transactions per student/person in the area service population
- e-book downloads
- e-book downloads per student/person in the area service population
- reference transactions per student/person in the area service population
- services and programs offered, especially those unduplicated by any other organization or institution in the same geopolitical area
- program attendance per student/person in the area service population
- public internet computer use per student/person in the area service population
- total library expenditures
- total library expenditures per student/person in the area service population
- total library materials expenditures
- total library materials expenditures per student/person in the area service population
- ratio of interlibrary loan items loaned to items borrowed
- volumes held per student/person in the area service population
- titles held per student/person in the area service population
- number of databases licensed for access
- number of full-text serial titles, unduplicated, accessible via the databases or through the library's catalog
- unique collections, such as those in the library's special collections or archives
- percentage of collections converted to digital formats to increase access, and the external awareness of unique content

CHAPTER SIX

Net Promoter Score

1. Calculate the Net Promoter Score (NPS): (Note: the data included in the chapter question—for 2011, 2012, and part of 2013—might be displayed as bar charts).

- 2011

  Promoters (549 + 2130) = 2679

  Detractors (9 + 4 + 9 + 13 + 53 + 112) = 200

  2679 + 200 = 2879

  $$NPS = \frac{2679}{2879} - \frac{200}{2879} =$$

  NPS = 93.1% − 6.9% =

  NPS = 86.2%

- 2012

  Promoters (514 + 2012) = 2526

  Detractors (15, 7, 12, 18, 62, 119) = 233

  2526 + 233 = 2759

  $$NPS = \frac{2526}{2759} - \frac{233}{2759} =$$

  NPS = 91.6% − 8.4% =

  NPS = 83.2%

- January–June 2013

  Promoters (314 + 1002) = 1316

  Detractors (7 + 4 + 6 + 11 + 44 + 61) = 133

  1316 = 133 = 1449

  $$NPS = \frac{1316}{1449} - \frac{133}{1449} =$$

  NPS = 90.8% − 9.2% =

  NPS = 81.6%

Summary Table

	2011	2012	2013 (JAN.-JUNE)
NPS	86.2%	83.2%	81.6%

2. There is a decline. Still, there is an opportunity to improve for the remainder of 2013. Two questions should be considered: (1) Is the percentage of decline important? (2) What are the reasons for the decline? To answer the second question we turn to the Opportunity Index.

3. This is a discussion question, one that does not lend itself to one answer. However, as managers address it, they should consider the extent to which they practice transparency with the staff and customers. They might consider the use of dashboards on the library's home page; see Robert E. Dugan, Peter Hernon, and Danuta A. Nitecki, *Engaging in Evaluation and Assessment Research* (Santa Barbara, CA: Libraries Unlimited, 2011), 175–76, 195–96.

   The next two questions, "How well do these services compare to your expectations?" and "Overall how do you rate the quality of these services?" deal with services and relate expectations to actual performance. As a result, they are comparable and subject to analysis using the NPS:

   - "How well do these services compare to your expectations?"

     Promoters (662 + 957) = 1619

     Detractors (28 + 42 + 57 + 75 + 164 + 296) = 662

     1619 = 662 = 2281

     $$NPS = \frac{1619}{2281} - \frac{662}{2281} =$$

     NPS = 71% − 29% =

     NPS = 42%

- "Overall how do you rate the quality of these services?"

Promoters (678 + 1029) = 1707

Detractors (23 + 33 + 40 + 59 + 118 + 230) = 503

1707 + 503 = 2210

$$\text{NPS} = \frac{1707}{2210} - \frac{503}{2210} =$$

NPS = 77.2% − 22.8% =

NPS = 54.4%

We would think that library managers would be concerned about NPSs of 42% and 54.4%. It may be unsatisfactory merely to review the Opportunity Index. Instead, they may call for focus group interviews to explore the issues in some depth. For an overview of focus group interviews see Peter Hernon and Ellen Altman, *Assessing Service Quality: Satisfying the Expectations of Library Customers* (Chicago: American Library Association, 2010), 111–15.

Opportunity Index

4. Step one: the mean for question 1 is 26.5 (265/10 =) and the mean for step two is 25.7 (257/10 =). Next, 26.5 + 26.5 = 53 and 53 − 25.7 = 27.3

Step two (the question about hours of access and operations). Importance: the mean is 19.7 (197/10 =) and satisfaction: the mean is 17.1 (171/10 =). Next, 19.7 + 19.7 = 39.4. And 39.4 − 17.1 = 22.3. Note that the value of 22.3 is less than 39.4; thus, the item about hours of access and operation would not be included in the index.

Recommend Rate

5–7: • 2011

Promoters: 512 + 1767 = 2279

Everyone else: 28 + 27 + 29 + 39 + 85 + 180 + 167 + 349 = 904

2279 + 904 = 3183

$$\text{Recommended Rate} = \frac{2279}{3183} - \frac{904}{3183} =$$

Recommended Rate = 71.6% − 28.4% =

Recommended Rate = 43.2%

- 2012

  Promoters: 347 + 2651 = 2998

  Everyone else: 33 + 39 + 18 + 14 + 82 + 130 + 181
  + 153 = 650

  2998 + 650 = 3648

  $$\text{Recommended Rate} = \frac{2998}{3648} - \frac{650}{3648} =$$

  Recommended Rate = 82.2% − 17.8% =

  Recommended Rate = 64.4%

- January–June 2013

  Promoters: 33 + 798 = 831

  Everyone else: 19 + 17 + 24 + 12 + 29 + 168 + 22
  + 99 = 390

  831 + 390 = 1221

  $$\text{Recommended Rate} = \frac{831}{1221} - \frac{390}{1221} =$$

  Recommended Rate = 68.1% − 31.9% =

  Recommended Rate = 36.2%

Summary Table

	2011	2012	2013 (JAN.–JUNE)
Recommended Rate	43.2%	64.4%	36.2%

8. The above table documents a volatile situation, one that managers should not ignore. It is important to identify the reasons and take corrective action. How would you go about ascertaining the reasons? However, the assumption is that the rate is poor. Do you

agree? Discuss (remember, any metric must be placed in some context).

9. Would you share this information throughout the organization and with your community? Discuss.

Reuse Rate

10–12: • 2011

Promoters: 333 + 2245 = 2578

Everyone else: 21 + 24 + 23 + 22 + 66 + 135 + 91 + 187 = 568

2578 + 568 = 3147

Reuse Rate $= \frac{2578}{3147} - \frac{568}{3147} =$

Reuse Rate = 81.9% − 18.1% =

Reuse Rate = 63.8%

• 2012

Promoters: 353 + 2500 = 2853

Everyone else: 17 + 19 + 20 + 16 + 75 + 140 + 81 + 173 = 541

2853 + 541 = 3394

Reuse Rate $= \frac{2853}{3394} - \frac{541}{3394} =$

Reuse Rate = 84.1% − 15.9% =

Reuse Rate = 68.2%

• January–June 2013

Promoters: 137 + 1098 = 1235

Everyone else: 16 + 13 + 21 + 14 + 26 + 134 + 37 + 99 = 360

1235 + 360 = 1595

$$\text{Reuse Rate} = \frac{1235}{1595} - \frac{360}{1595} =$$

Reuse Rate = 74.4% − 22.6% =

Reuse Rate = 51.8%

Summary Table*

	2011	2012	2013 (JAN.–JUNE)
Reuse Rate	63.8%	68.2%	51.8%

* However, the assumption might be that the rate is poor. Do you agree? Discuss (remember, any metric must be placed in some context).

13. Some managers may not like to base the recommend and reuse rates on a comparison of promoters to all others because the resulting percentage may be lower than they would prefer. Instead, they might want to calculate and report the mean score for each year. However, this method does not deal with the basic feature of the NPS, namely promoters and detractors. Therefore, other managers may prefer to ignore passives and base both rates on the percentage of promoters—the percentage of detractors.

    From 2011 to 2012, there is an increase in the percentage, and the remaining part of 2013 represents an opportunity to increase the rate. Focus group interviews and exit interviews might be a supplemental way to study both rates and to determine the reasons behind them.

14. The display might be on the home page and in the form of a dashboard. Of course, there are other options, some less public than others.

Resolution Rate

15. First, of the 123 customers offering comments, 10 + 29 (39, 31.7%) provided contact information. Of the 10 (completing comment card), five are critical of their visit and, of the 29, 15 are critical. Of the five, three later expressed satisfaction with the resolution of the matter (3 divided by 5, 60%) and, of the 15, 10 expressed satisfaction with the resolution of the matter (10 divided by 15, 66.6%). Viewed another way, the resolution rate is 13 divided by 20, 65%.

Clearly, any reporting of the resolution rate requires some explanation.

Analysis of box 6.3 will reveal patterns such as mention of the homeless that might reflect two perspectives, that of the homeless themselves and of other customers.

CHAPTER SEVEN

1. There is no single answer to this question. Any library should make its own determination.

2. Both service quality and satisfaction are derived from the Gaps Model of Service Quality and relate to customer expectations. Satisfaction can be explored overall or for a particular library "visit" or experience, whereas service quality is more global and deals with service statements that if deemed important to library customers, the library is willing to elevate to a high priority and meet on a constant basis. These statements most likely shift and do not remain static. Thus, it is important for libraries to settle on the statements for which they want customer input.

3. With customer service libraries do not attempt to meet all expectations; rather they set priorities and within those priorities service quality statements arise. Those statements are intended to make the customer experience more successful and pleasant. For a discussion of customer service and how service quality fits in, see Peter Hernon and Ellen Altman, *Assessing Service Quality: Meeting the Expectations of Library Customers* (Chicago: American Library Association, 2010).

4. The answer involves a judgment call and consideration in terms of the individual library.

5. There is no single answer to this question. Readers have many choices about the selection of metrics.

6. "Yes." They might explore facilities use (e.g., clean facilities or availability of parking) or use of technology (e.g., circulation of laptops, use of computer terminals, extent to which equipment is

not operational, or use of specific furniture). As part of the answer, managers should not forget to consider those with disabilities.

CHAPTER EIGHT

The questions are ones for discussion as there is no single or simple answer that applies to all libraries.

CHAPTER NINE

The questions are ones for discussion as there is no single or simple answer that applies to all libraries. Individual libraries might even take peer or competitive organizations into account when answering the questions.

CHAPTER TEN

1. The differing stakeholders will best respond to differing communications means, content, and presentations:

    Library staff: staff will respond to both a written report and a face-to-face presentation of the results. They want to know how the results will be used, especially if it means revising their current job responsibilities or functions. The presenter can expect questions following the presentation.

    Friends' group: because of the work the Friends do as volunteers and helping to raise funds, they are worthy of a face-to-face presentation. They are going to want to see a direct link between the funds raised and their use, particularly that the funds were not diverted to other projects unless the terms of the funds raised enable library managers to expend the revenue at the library's discretion.

    Prospective donors: may be initially approached with a brochure highlighting the successes the library has had with donations—linking donated funds to specific projects, and the impact on users as a result of these funded projects. The library may want to present the prospective donor with a "wish list" at a face-to-face meeting based upon the needs of the library aligned with the interests of the donor; this personal approach may help secure a donation.

Boards of trustees: the responsibilities for trustees vary by institution and may range from policy review and governance to ensuring the public's trust as financial stewards. The board will be familiar with the inputs; they will be most interested in how these inputs were used to produce outputs that meet the need of the users, and outcomes demonstrating the library's effect on individuals. This should include charts of inputs and outputs. For example, $10,000 was funded for monographs. The outputs would be that the library added 100 titles to its monographs collections, and the users borrowed 50,000 books during the past fiscal year. They would also expect to review trend analysis for the past five to ten years. Although most boards are comprised of laymen, trustees will "tolerate and endure" more of the technical information in their scheduled meetings than most other stakeholder groups other than library staff.

Institutional stakeholders: this group includes those overseeing the management of the library at the institutional level, as well as community governing boards and local media. Many of these stakeholders would be interested in the financial status of the library, including the alignment of inputs to outputs, and an indication of how the outputs affected individuals and groups. They would also be interested in learning about the financial stewardship of the library as well as the efficiencies the library realized during the fiscal year. Stories about individual and group successes achieved would also be of interest. The means to communicate would include short written monthly reports that accrue to a larger and more detailed written annual report. These stakeholders will also scan the local media for library events (e.g., "it's Tax Tuesday, and advisors will be at the library to answer questions about this year's federal and state tax returns") and stories as told by users (e.g., "I used the computers at the library to apply for jobs—and I found one!"). They are seeking to learn about, and understand, the link between the resources allocated to the library and their application to provide services aligned with the institution's mission successfully. A successful year may be rewarded by the library being asked to present its story face-to-face to some of the stakeholder groups.

State legislators: most states provide direct and indirect assistance to academic and public libraries. State legislators are always looking to be seen with "winners." Therefore, the library may want to send the state legislators brief public relations materials about events and programs in their libraries that are supported with state funds. Additionally, librarians should try to meet with their state legislators at least once a year to thank them for their support, tell them about these successes, and to seek continuation of the support they provide. It is not likely that many librarians will present before convened legislative financial committees, but it is possible that the state librarian and/or director of the state library administrative agency will be called upon to present and defend the annual fiscal year budget request. Library success stories, as well as examples of financial stewardship, will help make the case for continued state support.

Users: the means as well as the content of the communications will be as varied as the users themselves. Public library users will want to know about the library's busyness explained within a relative context. For example, they would be interested in knowing that more people used the library than went to the movies in the city. They also like knowing the dollar value returned; such as users collectively borrowed $1,000,000 worth of books or that the average family borrowed $100 worth of DVDs while they only expended $50 of their local taxes to support the library. The library may want to make available a web-based library use value calculator so that users may learn how they directly benefit from "taking advantage" of the library. The means to communicate should include a library newsletter in print, via the website, and available through e-mail or an RSS feed, and flyers or brochures providing the users with "the library by the numbers" information, and access to both the executive summary as well as the full version of the library's submitted annual report. The library may also want to host a "state of the library" night to talk about successes and respond to questions from the public. Academic users want to know what the library can do to help them; faculty want to know about resources available and sometimes about their cost and use, while students also want to know about the assistance available and the library's hours open. The academic library's website is an important communication means. Faculty and students do not have much interest in formal written annual reports, but are sometimes interested in the usage and cost information if brief and presented graphically for a quick perusal via the website, on posters hanging in library areas with extraordinary foot traffic, and in printed brochures or flyers.

2. A pie chart.

CHAPTER ELEVEN

The questions are ones for discussion as there is no single or simple answer that applies to all libraries. Individual libraries might even take peer or competitive organizations into account when answering the questions.

SELECTED READINGS

Communicating Results

Hernon, Peter, Robert E. Dugan, and Danuta Nitecki. *Engaging in Evaluation and Assessment Research.* Santa Barbara, CA: Libraries Unlimited, 2011.

Klass, Gary M. *Just Plain Data Analysis: Finding, Presenting, and Interpreting Social Science Data.* Lanham, MD: Rowman & Littlefield, 2008.

Customer Expectations (Satisfaction and Service Quality)

Hernon, Peter, and Ellen Altman. *Assessing Service Quality: Satisfying the Expectations of Library Customers*, 2nd ed. Chicago: American Library Association, 2010.

Hernon, Peter, and Joseph R. Matthews. *Listening to the Customer.* Santa Barbara, CA: Libraries Unlimited, 2011.

Evidence-Based Planning and Decision Making

Booth, Andrew. "Evaluating Your Performance." In *Evidence-Based Practice for Information Professionals: A Handbook*, edited by Andrew Booth and Anne Brice, 127–37. London: Facet Publishing, 2004.

Booth, Andrew, and Anne Brice. "Appraising the Evidence." In *Evidence-Based Practice for Information Professionals: A Handbook*, edited by Andrew Booth and Anne Brice, 104–18. London: Facet Publishing, 2004.

Crumley, Ellen, and Denise Koufogiannakis. "Developing Evidence-Based Librarianship: Practical Steps for Implementation." *Health Information and Libraries Journal* 19, no. 2 (2002): 61–70.

Grefsheim, Suzanne F., Jocelyn A. Rankin, and Susan C. Whitmore. "Making a Commitment to EBLIP: The Role of Library Leadership." *Evidence Based Library and Information Practice* 2, no. 3 (2007): 123–29.

Koufogiannakis, Denise. "Considering the Place of Practice-Based Evidence within Evidence Based Library and Information Practice (EBLIP)," *Library and Information Research* 35, no. 111 (2011): 41–58.

Metrics

Brophy, Peter. *Measuring Library Performance: Principles and Techniques*. London: Facet Publishing, 2006.

Dugan, Robert E., Peter Hernon, and Danuta A. Nitecki. *Viewing Library Metrics from Different Perspective: Inputs, Outputs and Outcomes*. Santa Barbara, CA: Libraries Unlimited, 2009.

Gratch Lindauer, Bonnie. "Defining and Measuring the Library's Impact on Campuswide Outcomes." *College & Research Libraries* 59, no. 6 (November 1998): 546–70.

Pritchard, Sarah M. "Determining Quality in Academic Libraries." *Library Trends* 44, no. 3 (Winter 1996): 572–94.

Urquhart, Christine. "How Do I Measure the Impact of My Service?" In *Evidence-Based Practice for Information Professionals: A Handbook*, edited by Andrew Booth and Anne Brice, 210–22. London: Facet Publishing, 2004.

Return on Investment

Berk & Associates. *Providing for Knowledge, Growth, and Prosperity: A Benefit Study of the San Francisco Public Library*. Seattle, WA: Berk & Associates, 2007.

———. *The Seattle Public Library Central Library: The Transforming Power of a Library to Redefine Learning, Community, and Economic Development*. Seattle, WA: Berk & Associates, 2005.

Carnegie Mellon University, Center for Economic Development. *Carnegie Library of Pittsburgh: Community Impact and Benefits*. Pittsburgh, PA: Carnegie Mellon University, 2006.

Elliott, Donald S., Glen E. Holt, Sterling E. Hayden, and Leslie E. Holt. *Measuring Your Library's Value: How to Do a Cost-Benefit Analysis for Your Public Library*. Chicago: American Library Association, 2007.

Florida Department of State. *Florida's Public Libraries Build Strong Economies: A Taxpayer Return on Investment Report.* Tallahassee, FL: Florida Department of State, 2005.

Fraser, Bruce T., Timothy W. Nelson, and Charles R. McClure. "Describing the Economic Impacts and Benefits of Florida Public Libraries: Findings and Methodological Applications for Future Work." *Library & Information Science Research* 24, no. 3 (2002): 211–33.

Griffiths, Jose-Marie, Donald W. King, and Sarah Aerni. *Taxpayer Return-on-Investment (ROI) in Pennsylvania Public Libraries.* Chapel Hill: University of North Carolina, School of Information and Library Science, 2006.

Griffiths, Jose-Marie, Donald W. King, C. Tomer, T. Lynch, and J. Harrington. *Taxpayer Return-on-Investment in Florida Public Libraries: Summary Report* (2004). For this and other ROI reports from the Florida Department of State, Division of Libraries & Information Services, http://dlis.dos.state.fl.us/bld/roi/publications.cfm.

King, Donald. "Demonstration of Methods to Assess the Use, Value, and ROI of All Academic Library Services" (2012). Available from http://libvalue.cci.utk.edu/content/lib value publications presentations reports.

"Making Book: Gambling on the Future of Our Libraries: Executive Summary of the KC Consensus White Paper" (2004). www.haplr-index.com/Making%20Book%20KCConsensus%20Library%20report-execsum.pdf.

Matthews, Joseph R. "What's the Return on ROI? The Benefits and Challenges of Calculating Your Library's Return on Investment." *Library Leadership & Management* 25, no. 1 (2011): 1–14.

"META Project—Valuation Studies: Valuation Studies of American Public Libraries" (2009). www.libsci.sc.edu/metaweb/valuationstudies.html.

Mott, Linn. "Cost-Benefit Analysis: A Primer." *Bottom Line: Managing Library Finances* 23, no. 1 (2010): 31–36.

Public Agenda Foundation. *Long Overdue: A Fresh Look at Public Attitudes about Libraries in the 21st Century.* New York: Public Agenda Foundation, 2006.

University of West Florida, Haas Center for Business Research and Economic Development. "Taxpayer Return on Investment in Florida Public Libraries" (May 2010), http://haas.uwf.edu/library/library_study/DraftFinal.pdf.

Urban Libraries Council. *Making Cities Stronger: Public Library Contributions to Local Economic Development.* Chicago: Urban Libraries Council, 2007.

Value

Association of College and Research Libraries. *Value of Academic Libraries: A Comprehensive Research Review and Report,* prepared by Megan Oakleaf. Chicago: Association of College and Research Libraries, 2010.

Elliott, Donald S., Glen E. Holt, Sterling E. Hayden, and Leslie E. Holt. *Measuring Your Library's Value: How to Do a Cost-Benefit Analysis for Your Public Library.* Chicago: American Library Association, 2007.

Friends of the San Francisco Public Library. *Providing for Knowledge, Growth and Prosperity: A Benefit Study of the San Francisco Public Library,* prepared by Berk and Associates (2007). http://sfpl.org/pdf/news/benefitstudy2007.pdf.

Georgia Public Library. "The Economic Value of Public Libraries: a Bibliography" (2007). www.georgialibraries.org/lib/collection/econ_value_bib.php.

Hernon, Peter, and Ellen Altman. *Assessing Service Quality: Satisfying the Expectations of Library Customers,* pp. 39–40. Chicago: American Library Association, 2010.

King, Donald. *Demonstration of Methods to Assess the Use, Value, and ROI of All Academic Library Services* (2012). Available from http://libvalue.cci.utk.edu/content/lib-value-publications-presentations-reports.

Markless, Sharon, and David Streatfield. *Evaluating the Impact of Your Library.* London: Facet Publishing, 2006.

Nystrom, Viveca, and Linnea Sjogren. *An Evaluation of the Benefits and Value of Libraries.* London: Chandos Publishing, 2012.

Saracevic, Tefko, and Paul B. Kantor. "Studying the Value of Library and Information Services: Part I, Establishing a Theoretical Framework." *Journal of the American Society of Information Science* 48, no. 6 (1997): 527–42.

———. "Studying the Value of Library and Information Services: Part II, Methodology and Taxonomy." *Journal of the American Society of Information Science* 48, no. 6 (1997): 543–63.

University of Pennsylvania, Fels Institute of Government, Fels Research & Consulting. *The Economic Value of the Free Library in Philadelphia* (2010). www.freelibrary.org/about/Fels_Report.pdf.

ABOUT THE AUTHORS

Robert E. Dugan is the dean of libraries at the University of West Florida (Pensacola, FL). Prior to assuming this position, he had been at Suffolk University, Boston; Wesley College, Dover, DE; and Georgetown University, Washington, DC. He has also worked in state and public libraries during his nearly forty-year career. He is the coauthor of eleven books, including the award-winning *Viewing Library Metrics from Different Perspectives* (2009).

Peter Hernon is a professor at Simmons College (Graduate School of Library and Information Science, Boston) and the principal faculty member for the doctoral program, Managerial Leadership in the Information Professions. He received his PhD degree from Indiana University, Bloomington, was the 2008 recipient of the Association of College and Research Libraries' award for Academic/Research Librarian of the Year, is the coeditor of *Library & Information Science Research*, and has taught, conducted workshops, and delivered addresses in ten countries outside the United States. He is the author or coauthor of fifty-five books, including the award-winning *Federal Information Policies in the 1980s* (1985), *Assessing Service Quality* (1998), and *Viewing Library Metrics from Different Perspectives* (2009).

Joseph R. Matthews is a consultant specializing in strategic planning, assessment, evaluation of library services, customer service, use of performance metrics, and the balanced scorecard. He was an instructor at the San Jose State University School of Library and Information Science. He is the author of *The Customer-Focused Library* (2009), *The Evaluation and Measurement of Library Services* (2007), *Scorecards for Results* (2008), *Strategic Planning and Management for Managers* (2005), and *Measuring for Results* (2003), and the coauthor (with Peter Hernon) of *Reflecting on the Future of Academic and Public Libraries* (2013) and *Listening to the Customer* (2011), among other books.

INDEX

A

academic libraries
  comparisons and, 68
  evaluation questions and, 11
  external evaluations and, 80, 87, 89 92
  internal evaluations and, 49–50
  metrics and, 36–39
  partnerships and, 87
  reputation and, 95
  value of, 161–162
access, direct use benefits and, 143
accountability
  creating change and, 191
  dashboard, 181
  evidence based planning and, 17 18
  library stakeholders and, 73–74
accreditation support, 77, 90–91
accuracy
  evaluation questions and, 10
  metrics and, 35
ACRLMetrics, 38
administration and management, 80–85
administrative agencies, 175–176
affect, results and value, 159–160
affect of service, 129

aggregate value, 140
Altman, Ellen, 6, 36, 106–107
American Customer Satisfaction Index, 114
analysis
  complaint/compliment, 104–106
  data collection methods and, 104–107
  evidence-based planning and, 24–25
  full text tools, 131
  Gap analysis, 22
  mechanisms for, 51
  multiplier, 148
  quantitative mechanisms, 51, 54
  return on investment and, 149–151
  ROI type, 138
articles, 183
Assessing Service Quality (Hernon and Altman), 37, 106
assessments, 3, 23–24, 93
Association of College and Research Libraries (ACRL), 37
Association of Research Libraries (ARL), 38, 130–132
assurance, surveys and, 129
austerity, creating change and, 191